Women's Work and Family Values, 1920-1940

Library of Congress Cataloging in Publication Data

Wandersee, Winifred D
    Women's work and family values, 1920-1940.

    Bibliography: p.
    Includes index.
        1.   Wives—Employment—United States.   2.   House-
wives—United States.   3.   Cost and standard of
living—United States.   4.   United States—Economic
conditions—1918—1945.   I.   Title.
HD6055.2.U6W36   331.4'3'0973   80-21100
ISBN 0-674-95535-8

Women's Work and Family Values

1920-1940

Winifred D. Wandersee

Harvard University Press

Cambridge, Massachusetts, and London, England   1981

Acknowledgments

Many people have been a source of intellectual and moral support while I worked on this project. Two outstanding contributors were Clarke A. Chambers and John Modell of the University of Minnesota. They offered scholarly advice and personal encouragement over the years I was writing this book. Their enthusiasm for scholarship in general and for my topic in particular gave me the confidence and the freedom to pursue the research along my own lines of inquiry.

Lynn Weiner of Boston University, who read the original and revised manuscripts, provided intellectual stimulation and valuable advice based upon her own insights as a historian of women and work. More important, her friendship was a source of much-needed moral support. Similarly, Lois Scharf, who has recently completed an important work on the 1930s, provided intellectual stimulation and professional advice, as well as constant friendship.

Aida DiPace Donald of Harvard University Press conveyed an interest in my work from the beginning, which made it possible for me to undertake a difficult but rewarding revision of the original manuscript. Virginia LaPlante took on the task of editing the manuscript and seeing that I met the necessary deadlines.

This study was completed during a year of personal and professional transition of considerable magnitude. For that reason, my emotional indebtedness is great. I am grateful to Gretchen Kreuter of the College of St. Catherine, St. Paul, Minnesota, for her professional advice, emotional support, and constant assurance that I was "making it." My parents, Dorothy and Fred Wandersee, historians in their own right, and my brother, Richard Wandersee, have helped me in more ways than I can express. I am also grateful to the support of two different groups of friends—one in the Minneapolis-St. Paul area, the other at Syracuse University. Though too numerous to name, these people know who they are and what they have done.

I would like to express thanks for permission to use parts of the article "The Economics of Middle-Income Family Life: Working Women During the Great Depression," *Journal of American History* 65 (June 1978):60-74, and parts of the essay "American Women and the Twentieth Century Work Force: The Depression Experience," in Mary Kelley, ed., *Women, Identity and Vocation in American History* (G. K. Hall, 1979).

Finally, I am dedicating this book to three young people—Wes, Ben, and Andrea Bolin—who have impressed me with their courage and maturity.

Contents

Introduction   *1*

1   **The Economics of Family Life**   *7*

2   **Deficit Living**   *27*

3   **Mothers and Children**   *55*

4   **The Married Woman Worker**   *67*

5   **Working Women in the Great Depression**   *84*

6   **Women's Place in the Home**   *103*

Epilogue   *118*

Appendixes   *125*
Bibliography   *133*
Notes   *141*
Index   *162*

TABLES

1.1   Distribution of family income, 1929   10
2.1   Distribution of family income, 1935-1936   34
2.2   Distribution of family income, 1929 and 1935-1936   34
2.3   Distribution of income among families and unattached individuals,
      1929-1944   35
2.4   Passenger automobiles and gasoline sold, 1929-1936   42
3.1   Urban and rural nonfarm families by earners and family
      income, 1939   60
3.2   Percentage of children 10-15 years old of both sexes in the labor
      force, 1880-1930   61
3.3   Percentage of children 14-19 years old of both sexes in the labor
      force, 1900-1940   62
3.4   Persons other than head of household in the labor force by age and
      sex, 1940   63
3.5   Persons other than head of household in the labor force by class and
      occupation, 1940   64
4.1   Women in the labor force by marital condition, 1890-1940   68
4.2   Income of husbands of 652 gainfully employed women homemakers,
      1932   74
4.3   Income of husbands of women 18-64 years old with husband present,
      1939   79
4.4   Women workers in urban and rural nonfarm areas at each income level
      by income level of husband, 1939   80
4.5   Employment status and occupation of husbands of women 18-64 years
      old with husband present, 1940   82
5.1   Occupational distribution of female labor force, 1890-1930   85
5.2   Occupational distribution of female labor force, 1940   85
5.3   Distribution of female labor force by type of work, 1910-1940   89
5.4   Change in distribution of female labor force, 1910-1940   90
5.5   Married women workers over 14 years old, 1910, 1940   91
5.6   Women workers seeking employment by occupation, July 1936   93
B.1   Consumer installment credit and total consumer credit outstanding at
      end of year, 1929-1937   127
C.1   National, personal, and corporate savings, 1929-1939   129
C.2   Expenditures and savings of nonfarm families by income class,
      1935-1936   129

Women's Work and Family Values, 1920-1940

Introduction

In the history of women and work, the relationship between women's domestic roles and their work outside of the home was such that their labor force participation was a direct extension of their family roles.[1] Women's employment outside the home became increasingly necessary during the twentieth century as household production declined and consumption rose in importance in American family life. [For most women, outside work was a reflection of their commitment to family values rather than an indication of their shift in values toward autonomy or self-realization.] Although there were exceptions to this general pattern, and women often worked for a combination of reasons, the experience of most women workers was shaped by the economic realities of family life.

As a consequence of these realities, economic need motivated women to seek employment outside the home, and this is the way in which women have customarily defined their work roles. But economic need is a concept not easily measured. The issue of need cuts across class lines, and although the intensity of need varies, the phenomenon is dependent upon the particular values of individual families rather than the absolute requirements of daily survival.

One of the basic facts of family economics during the early decades of the twentieth century was that most working-class males, and many of those in the middle class, were not paid enough to support their families according to the American standard of living.[2] By the 1920s, the rise in consumerism, encouraged by high production and mass advertising, had affected the lives and attitudes of all Americans to some degree. Although many families lived in poverty, the definition of economic need for those above the poverty level was shaped by new ideas of what constituted an acceptable standard of living. [The term "standard of living" refers to a level of aspiration, and many families in the twentieth century have had a standard of living that they are unable to achieve on the income of one wage-earner. They either live beyond their means in an attempt to realize their standard, or they count on the contribution of a supplementary wage-earner. One or both of these patterns characterized many families in the 1920s and 1930s, and strongly influenced the labor force behavior of married women workers.

The movement of married women into the labor force, which became a significant trend during the 1920s and 1930s, signaled the beginning of a long-range cultural change that was rooted in the economic values of twentieth-century family life. The rise of bureaucracy, service industries, advertising, and mass consumption played an important role in influencing family values with respect to employment, standard of living, and the roles of women and children. The family was an integral part of the complexities of twentieth-century economic life, and family members participated in both the domestic sphere and the public marketplace. Early in the century, young people were most apt to be the supplementary wage-earner, but by the middle of the century, married women had supplanted them.

Married women who were gainfully employed during the 1920s and 1930s were always in the minority, and even among very low-income families there were never more than 25 percent of all wives gainfully employed. Black women were an exception to this rule in that they were rarely able to share the pattern of values that influenced white women to stay out of the labor force. About twice as high a proportion of black women were in the labor force as white women. The difference between the races went beyond mere economics to basic family values, for at every income level, black women were more likely to be gainfully employed than white women.[3]

Most married white women resisted gainful employment because, in spite of economic pressures, societal and domestic demands exerted an even greater influence. Housework and child care took up much of their time, and society did not provide the necessary services to lighten that load. Public opinion was also resistant to the employment of married women, jobs were rarely available, and the experience of most middle-class women led them to view outside work as an unattractive alternative to housework.

Those who were able and willing to adapt themselves to the interaction between economic and domestic roles usually did so for one of three reasons: their need was so great that they had little choice but to work, their employment opportunity was favorable, or their value system stressed the material comfort of the family at the expense of traditional concepts of women's role. The last two groups of women represented a change in family values, aimed at satisfying new needs rather than avoiding a poverty-level existence. But these women were able to rationalize their activities outside the home within the existing framework of traditional family values by defining their work in terms of the economic needs of the family.[4]

The difference between the minority of women who worked and the majority who did not was partly a difference in values, but also a difference in circumstances. The nonworking wife could become gainfully employed if the right set of circumstances converged with respect to economic need, employment opportunities, age of children, and attitude of the husband. Similarily, a working wife might drop out of the work force if she became pregnant, if her husband got a raise or a new job, or if she lost her job. No one factor was decisive in determining the labor force behavior of women as a group, but the growing flexibility in their tendency to work reflected changing attitudes toward family roles as well as an unshaken commitment to family responsibilities. [Although economic *Thesis* need was still the critical factor leading women to work, the changing definition of economic need was the result of new family values with respect to consumption, standard of living, and the role of women and children in the family.]

The economics of family life during the 1920s and 1930s were characterized by an increased emphasis on consumption and a new definition of economic need. The shift from the general prosperity of the twenties to the Depression of the thirties brought about a decline in consumption but did little to affect the actual values of families with respect to standard of living. In order to maintain the standards achieved during the 1920s, families often went into debt or resorted to supplementary wage-earners. Although many families had to follow these measures simply to survive, for a wide range of middle-income families the choice was based upon relative values rather than absolute need.

By the 1920s women's domestic role reflected new standards of living with respect to housekeeping duties and patterns of consumption, but it also reflected an increased emphasis on the mother-child relationship. The decline of child labor in the twentieth century, along with the extension of compulsory school attendence, lengthened and intensified childhood. Social and psychological theories which emphasized the importance of the early childhood years placed a heavy responsibility upon the mother as the primary parent shaping the child's development. For the mother who was also a wage-earner, this meant maintaining a dual role of child-rearing and wage-earning, duties that often conflicted with each other, although they both contributed to middle-class standards of family life.

Women's productive role outside the home was also affected by the occupational distribution of the labor force and the state of the economy. During the Great Depression women workers faced unemployment, and they also bore the burden of discrimination, which had the effect of retarding the movement of women into white collar and professional work. But by the end of the 1930s, in spite of adverse public opinion and employment policies, the proportion of married women workers had increased, and the married woman worker was now a reality of American economic life.

Whereas the productive function of married women changed markedly during the first four decades of the twentieth century, the change in their role or status in the home was less obvious. As household production decreased, some women filled their time with consumption, home management, and child-related activities. Others carried the double burden of productive work outside the home and domestic activities within it. Yet women's status in the family was not unaffected by the changing family values and related economic activities. The internal power structure of the family underwent changes in the twentieth century that were subtle, but nevertheless profound. In particular, the concept of "companionship" in marriage, which was related to changes in the economic and domestic sphere, had a positive effect on women's status, or at least on women's perception of that status, within the family. The 1930s had a special impact upon family roles, because the many men who were unemployed lost their power relative to that of women, who maintained their domestic roles and were sometimes even able to supersede their husbands as the primary wage-earner.[5]

Although the family was no longer a powerful political and economic institution, the change in women's family status, whether real or perceived, probably affected their attitude toward themselves and their role in a positive way. It may offer a partial explanation for women's lack of interest in or even hostility toward philosophies that challenged or threatened traditional family life. For example, feminism played a very small part in the developments of the interwar period.[6] Part of the failure of feminism can be attributed to the relatively narrow focus of the feminist debate during the 1920s and 1930s. The concentration on career versus marriage did not allow feminism to relate to the homemakers and working women who placed family first. Feminism, as a movement and an

ideology, failed during the pre-World War II years because it did not recognize the most essential characteristic of the great majority of American
women, their commitment to a traditional pattern of family life. To gain
a wide base of support, the feminist ideology would have had to adapt to
this reality. But the women's movement was rent by squabbles over the
Equal Rights Amendment, and that issue gave feminism a much nar-
rower focus than the women's movement of the presuffrage years, with
its emphasis upon social reform and progressive legislation, or than the
movement that was to emerge in the 1960s.

[The pattern of economic and social development that emerged in the
1920s and 1930s contributed to the current trends in American society.]
Although the women and families who during the interwar years accepted the dual role of the employed housewife were definitely in a
minority, they prefigured an important shift in family values and life-
styles that was to become dominant in the post-World War II years. By
the 1950s, American women had replaced young people as the most important supplementary wage-earner. Their participation in the work
force both reflected and contributed to the family's standard of living in a
period of affluence. But the values that underlay family economics during the postwar years of prosperity were present in the 1920s and were
sustained during the Depression of the 1930s.[7]

1

The Economics of Family Life

The interrelationship between cultural values and an economic system offers an intriguing and complex problem for the family. During the twentieth century American families faced economic developments that went beyond industrialism to affect their lives and values in direct and personal ways. Although industrialism remained a constant force in American society in the early decades of this century, the economy shifted its emphasis from industrial production to the production of consumer goods and services, communication systems, and mass advertising. The result was a corresponding shift in the nature of employment opportunities, as well as the emergence of a changing pattern of consumption that affected the values of nearly all American families.

The shift in the nature of employment had a direct effect on the character of the labor force and the training of its participants. The family was affected indirectly but significantly, as children were kept out of the labor force in order to remain in school, and wives and mothers began to move into white-collar jobs, filling positions in the shops, offices, and service industries of the nation.

The change in consumption patterns had a varied impact upon family life, since the response to this change was always limited by financial means. But by the 1920s, American economic and social life had become a reflection of what was commonly referred to as "the American standard of living."[1] It is doubtful that the average American could have described the precise meaning of the term "American standard of living," but nearly everyone agreed that it was attainable, highly desirable, and far superior to that of any other nation. Its nature varied according to social class and regional differences, but no matter where a family stood socially and financially, it was certain to have aspirations set beyond that stance. This was the great paradox posed by the material prosperity of the twentieth century: prosperity was conspicuously present, but it was always just out of reach, for nearly every family defined its standard of living in terms of an income that it hoped to achieve rather than the reality of the paycheck.

In terms of income level, material goods, and ability to consume, the American people increased their standard of living considerably in the years between the late nineteenth century and the 1920s. The most reliable measure of this increase in well-being was the rise in real income. During the period from the 1890s to 1926, in spite of a substantial increase in the cost of living, real wages more than kept pace. In 1926, some 14 million workers were earning 233 percent more in average hourly wages than the average of the 1890s, and they were 125 percent above the 1914 average. This was equivalent to an increase in purchasing power of 38 percent and 30 percent, respectively.[2]

Much of the increase in real full-time weekly earnings came after 1920. Similarly, the average annual money earnings of workers in urban industries showed the greatest gains after 1920.[3] Thus, the twenties were a period of prosperity in the sense that most wage-earners saw their standard of living rise appreciably as compared to the more moderate increases of previous decades. Yet in spite of this apparent prosperity, the economic problems of family life were a constant theme of both popular and scholarly writing. The fiction of the popular magazines, such as *The Saturday Evening Post, Collier's,* and *American Magazine,* bemoaned the fate of young couples unable to marry on the man's wage of $20 a week, while the regularly featured columns advised brides about how to manage a budget. In 1925, a young married woman wrote an anonymous account to *Harper's Magazine* in which she complained bitterly about the cost of family living in New York City. Even more significant than this personal account were the large number of readers who felt compelled to respond with letters, some of them agreeing with her lament, but most of them criticizing her extravagance.[4]

The twenties also witnessed the full blooming of the home economics movement and a virtual outpouring of textbooks on home management, as well as scholarly studies of the economic basis of family life. Economists, home economists, social workers, journalists, and private citizens, all expressed their concern over the high cost of living and the difficulty of making ends meet. As a writer in *Ladies' Home Journal* declared, it was time to put the American home upon a "business-like basis."[5]

The interest in budgeting was hardly a recent phenomenon, but it became greatly intensified in the 1920s as more and more families were operating in a money economy in which nearly everything that they consumed or possessed could be acquired only with money. The degree to which this was true varied according to the economic situation, the social class, and the geographical location of the particular family, but as William Ogburn pointed out, by the 1920s many of the productive functions of family life were being performed outside of the home.[6]

Nonetheless, with the rise in real income so much in evidence, it seems incongruous that so many Americans felt that they were barely making ends meet. The answer to this paradox lies in the simple fact that most of them were not making enough in real wages to fulfill either their needs or their desires, but they were often willing to skimp on their needs in order to pursue their desires. Thus, rising expectations were a part of the economics of family life.

Another problem was the unequal distribution of income throughout the American economy. A study done by the Brookings Institution revealed the inequality among American families in 1929. Out of more than 27 million families with two or more persons, 12 million, or more than 42 percent, had incomes under $1,500. These families had an aggregate income of about $10 billion, whereas at the other end of the income scale, the 36,000 families with income in excess of $75,000 had an aggregate income of $9.8 billion. This tiny number of families at the top of the income scale, or 0.1 percent of the total, received practically as much income as 42 percent of the families at the bottom of the scale (Table 1.1).

Although the inequities of distribution were obvious, a more important consideration was the value of a family income in terms of the comfort it could buy. In other words, what did it mean to live on an income of $1,500 in 1929? The Brookings Institution Study speculated that a family income of $2,000 may have been sufficient to supply the basic necessities, but this estimate must be high, because more than 11 million families, or 42 percent of the total, were below this income standard.[7]

Many studies of family expenditures were done during the early years of the twentieth century. A bibliography published in 1930 listed 180 studies of costs and standards of living in the United States, going back to 1869.[8] Nearly three-fourths of these works investigated urban wage-earning families, but by the 1920s there were also a number of studies of farm families and families of the professional class.[9] The estimates of these studies generally showed the cost of living at two levels—the minimum tolerable American standard, sometimes called the "subsistence minimum," and a higher "health and decency" standard. Before World War I, the maintenance of the first standard for a family of five required about $800 annually in the larger cities, but according to Paul H. Doug-

Table 1.1 Distribution of family income, 1929

Income level ($)	No. families (1,000s)	% at each level	Cumulative (%)
0	120	0.5	0.4
Under 500	1,982	7.2	7.6
500–1,000	3,797	13.8	21.5
1,000–1,500	5,754	21.0	42.4
1,500–2,000	4,701	17.1	59.5
2,000–2,500	3,204	11.6	71.2
2,500–3,000	1,988	7.2	78.4
3,000–3,500	1,447	5.3	83.7
3,500–4,000	993	3.6	87.3
4,000–4,500	718	2.6	89.9
4,500–5,000	514	1.9	91.8
Over 5,000	2,256	8.2	100.0
Total	27,474	100.0	

Source: Maurice Leven, Harold G. Moulton, and Clark Warburton, *America's Capacity to Consume* (Washington, D.C.: Brookings Institution, 1934), p. 54.

las, the average annual money earnings of industrial wage-earners ranged from about $560 in 1905 to $670 in 1915.[10]

The many budget studies done by social and government agencies should not be taken too literally, for there were many problems involved in defining an adequate level of income and expenditure for a variety of family types. For instance, some families had more than one wage-earner; others had additional sources of income, or "noncash" income; while most had either more or less than the "typical" three children under fourteen years of age. All families pass through developmental cycles, and the financial demands of family life are closely related to the particular state of development. Furthermore, as Hazel Kryk pointed out, the conclusions arrived at in studies of expenditure were often to be used by one side or the other in a wage dispute, so that the estimate of adequacy or inadequacy depended upon the bias of the investigator.[11]

During the early years of the century, the concept of income adequacy was changing in response to the social developments of the Progressive Era. The agitation for health and labor legislation, as well as for other kinds of social reform, resulted in governmental activity at all levels, directed toward collecting data on income expenditures, savings, and living conditions of workers and others, especially those who were, or were apt to become, public charges. There was general agreement by the 1920s that incomes should provide some of the comforts of life beyond the bare necessities of food, housing, and clothing. But there was little agreement as to what constituted a living wage. A summary of several budgets that were made up in the early twenties shows the range of estimated costs of living in terms of 1923 prices:

Standard	Five-person Family
Poverty level	$1,000-1,100
Subsistence minimum	1,100-1,400
Health and decency minimum	1,500-1,700
Comfort minimum	2,100[12]

If these estimates are accurate, it is apparent that most American families in the twenties were living below the level of comfort and, indeed, probably below the level of minimum health and decency. Perhaps no other occupational group was more aware of the inadequacy of family incomes than the social and welfare workers who served the wage-earning families of the large cities. One of the most complicated problems for relief agencies was determining an adequate standard of living for their clients. In 1925 the United Charities of Chicago employed Florence Nesbitt, an expert in cost of living, to revise a manual which served as a standard for the relief-giving procedures of that agency. Nesbitt and the Committee on Family Social Work defined the minimum standard very broadly to include everything necessary to make possible a high standard of physical, mental, and moral health and efficiency for adults, and the full physical, mental, and moral growth and development of children.[13]

Nesbitt and her committee prepared two budgets based on these principles—one for a minimum-standard dependent family, and the other for a self-supporting family, necessarily assuming more financial responsibility. Excluding rent and insurance, items that were too variable to determine, the estimated budget for a dependent family of mother and three children was $61.80 a month. The major items included were food at $33.20, clothing and toilet articles at $13.35, and various miscellaneous items such as recreation, education, health care, and household furnishing at $7.25. These amounts were only approximate and would vary according to particular needs, former standards of living, and whether or not the mother was employed regularly outside the home.

The minimum budget for a self-supporting family included extra expenses not incurred by the dependent family, such as medical expenses, schoolbooks, emergencies, unemployment, and responsibilities to church and charities or other organizations for civic and personal benefit. For a family of five—parents and three children—a total of $129.07 a month was estimated as a minimum budget. This included $54.00 for food, $22.90 for clothing and toilet articles, and $52.17 for miscellaneous items. In other words, the self-sufficient family was expected to spend almost as much on miscellaneous items as on food. Educational expenses were estimated at $3.00, recreational expenses, $4.00, and household furnishing, $7.00 a month.

The Chicago standard budget reflected the developing need for a standard allowing for growth and development beyond mere physical well-being. There were still wide disparities between the dependent-family budget and the self-supporting family budget, but as relief agencies came to recognize the importance of maintaining dependent families in a manner that exceeded mere subsistence, the minimum normal standard of living was raised. Some of the members of the Committee on Family Social Work questioned this increase, suggesting that perhaps the budget for dependent families offered a higher level than that which could be maintained by the families of independent unskilled wage-earners.[14]

In response, Leila Houghteling investigated a group of 467 families of unskilled laborers in Chicago. She found that the earnings in the unskilled and semiskilled groups varied greatly, ranging from approximately $800 a year to $2,200, but that the majority made less than $1,500 a year. In more than two-thirds of the families these earnings were insufficient to provide a standard of living equal to that provided by the Chicago budget for dependent families. The discrepancy was particularly significant because this group of laborers was unusually fortunate in that they had been regularly employed throughout the year 1924 and had, for the most part, been in the employ of their firms for several years.

Houghteling also noted that in the case of 355 families there were other sources of income, including the earnings of wives and children, payment from boarders and lodgers, income from property, sick benefits, borrowed money, and gifts from friends and relatives. The addition of these sources of income meant that a little more than one-half of the total number of families were able to maintain a standard equal to or above the estimated budget. But according to Houghteling, the use of these sources sometimes resulted in a lowered standard of living. For instance, in 108 families the mother worked, usually at a particularly arduous job: this often meant a sacrifice in the care of dependent children in the family. Houghteling also felt that the presence of boarders and lodgers in 100 of the families resulted in overcrowding, which lowered the standard of physical and moral well-being.[15]

Her opinion reflected the values of most of her contemporaries who were interested in domestic life. Social welfare workers in particular were critical of the pattern of boarding and lodging that was typical of many working-class and lower-middle-class families, and they tended to define it as an "evil." However, a recent study on the subject suggests that the practice performed a valuable function in allowing urban families to adapt to their social and economic environment.[16]

In conclusion, Houghteling pointed out that for more than two-thirds of the 302 families for whom comparisons could be made, the wages of the chief wage-earner were not sufficient to maintain a standard of living equal to that provided by the Chicago budget. In some cases the deficit was great, amounting to more than one-half of the man's earnings. When all sources of income were included, more than one-half of the families were able to meet the requirements of the budget, but 44.9 percent still fell below.[17]

Houghteling's work reinforced the virtue of the one-wage-earner family in which the father was able to support the family, the mother stayed in the home to care for the children, and the children were able to remain in school at least through high school. Like most of her contemporaries, she felt that the necessity for several wage-earners in a family was a social evil which had a demoralizing effect upon family life.

Writing from a similar perspective, Katharine Anthony noted earlier in the 1920s that less than half of the wage-earners' families in the United States were supported entirely by the earnings of the husband or father. In other cases the earnings of the mother and children were a necessary supplement.[18] By the late twenties, conditions were not much better. A report at the 1928 National Conference of Social Work observed that under the existing system of values, the income of unskilled and semi-skilled workers was simply not adequate, and many families were unable to attain the essential minimum living standard established by social agencies for dependent families. The report suggested either a wage increase or some method of centralized control of production and distribution.[19]

During this same year, Karl de Schweinitz, head of the Philadelphia Society for Organizing Charity, reported the contrast between the prosperity of a large and resourceful city and the pitifully meager relief given to dependent families. The Family Society of Philadelphia had made a study of the wage-earnings of 552 households that had applied to it for help in 1925. When de Schweinitz compared the wages to the cost of living schedules of the Bureau of Municipal Research, he found that in approximately 88 percent of the 552 families the men were earning less than the necessary minimum wage of $38.35 a week for a family of five. In 119 of these families the mother or children, or both, were working at the time of application to the society. Lodgers or relatives were living in 81 families, which tended to increase the income of the households. But other factors were also operating to decrease income. For instance, most laborers did not work full-time year-round. Forty weeks out of fifty-two was considered to be the average annual employment of men in the building trades. Many workers were dependent upon weather conditions, and there were losses due to part-time work and layoffs. Furthermore, whereas the Bureau of Municipal Research assumed a family of three children, in the group of families studied there were as many households with more than three children as there were with less than three.[20]

The inequitable system of distribution was only a part of the economics of the twenties. The other side of the story was the rising expectations of a consumer-oriented society. Although Americans of all classes were living at a higher level than ever before, they had come to expect it, and there was little in the American economic system, with its rapidly increasing productivity, emphasis on consumer goods, mass advertising, and consumer credit system, to discourage this attitude. If the lower class of workers was dissatisfied with its lot, the middle class was not much better off in terms of fulfilling its aspirations. Many people in the business and professional class felt that their standard of living was not keeping pace with the development and prosperity of the nation. They felt that they had to struggle for the amenities of life, and they found it difficult on $3,000 a year to maintain a middle-class existence, living in a good neighborhood and providing educational opportunities for their children.[21]

Most middle-class families did not allow for the unexpected crisis in their budgeting. The woman, as the primary consumer in the family, often received the most criticism for the financial disorder of the home. As Anthony drily observed: "the preaching of thrift to the American housewife goes on incessantly by apostles from a business which is largely organized on the assumption that she does not possess it and which would be highly disconcerted if she actually developed it. American business loves the housewife for the same reason it loves China—that is, for her economic backwardness."[22]

The consumer society is sometimes seen as part and parcel of urban America, yet the values of consumerism spread to the rural areas in a way that was eventually to ease the clash between tradition and modernism. One of the most apparent social and economic problems of the decade was the lag of rural areas in per capita income and standard of living without a corresponding lag in what the farmers expected of life. With the increased contact between city and country owing to the telephone, radio, automobile, and mass advertising, farmers were beginning to feel themselves a part of the urbanized society. A standard of living is psychological as well as physical, so that it was natural for the rural areas to try to emulate the cities in their expectations. Farmers also wanted the convenience of electrical appliances and the pleasures of the radio.[23]

The new emphasis on consumerism was related to gains in productivity as well as gains in real wages. Marketing of goods superseded production as an economic problem, since it became crucial to maintain aggregate demand to match the output of goods and services. As William E. Leuchtenberg put it, the United States was "confronted with the need to fashion instruments and attitudes appropriate to an economy of abundance."[24]

Many of the attitudinal conflicts of the 1920s can be traced directly to the economy of abundance and the problem of distribution, the solution of which often resulted in a conflict of values. The "scarcity psychology" of the nineteenth century, with its emphasis on hard work, thrift, and capital accumulation, had come under attack before the 1920s, but during this decade it finally gave way to an "abundance psychology," capable of wasteful consumption of surplus products and wasteful use of leisure time. This social triumph was not achieved without a struggle, it would receive a setback in the thirties, and among certain groups and individuals it has never been completely successful; but it well reflected the dominant attitudinal climate of the twenties.

David Riesman remarked that his "other-directed" man, socialized to the new and freer ways of consumption by association with his peers and by the influence of the mass media, first emerged during this decade, as a product of the economy of abundance.[25] But Reisman's "inner-directed" predecessor did not simply disappear, and the resulting conflict of values between these two social types often made themselves felt within the family. Robert Lynd noted that "the tradition that rigorous saving and paying cash are the marks of sound family economy and personal self-respect" often clashed with "the new gospel which encourages liberal spending to make the wheels of industry turn as a duty of a citizen."[26]

Lynd argued that the problem of spending available money had become a complicating factor in urban family life, not only because of the growing array of goods and services, but also because of increasing individualism on the part of family members. The utilization of goods and services was passing from total-family consumption to consumption by individuals—men, women, boys, and girls, of different ages and personality needs. Family members, as their status and roles became more a matter of personality rights of the individual, constituted less of a unit than in any previous period in American history. American culture, with its emphasis on the health of business rather than the quality of family life, encouraged irrationality of consumption through advertising, thereby contributing to family conflict and even disintegration.[27]

Certainly advertising played a large part in developing high-level mass consumption in the twenties. The total dollar volume of advertising grew from $1,468 million in 1918 to $3,426 million in 1929. The increase was even more spectacular when considered in per capita terms. In 1919 the per capita expenditure on newspaper and periodical advertising was $5.03. By 1929, at the height of prosperity, the figure was up to $9.22, although it dipped quickly to $7.00 in 1931.[28]

The growth of advertising was a response to a number of developments, including a communication gap between producers and consumers, the variety of new merchandise on the market, product differentiation, the widening of the market through improved transportation, and increased recognition by businessmen of the value of advertising as a means of building demand. Advertising increased quantitatively, but it also changed qualitatively, playing upon the emotions, fears, and anxieties of Americans. That is, people's social insecurities made them susceptible to manipulation by advertisements that promised them status and security through consumption.[29]

The individualism that Lynd thought he saw in the consumption habits of family members was rather limited. Although consumers may have been concerned with their own personal needs, their purchasing decisions were becoming "massed decisions" rather than individual discriminating choices. Advertising, in its appeal to the largest number, strengthened the tendency toward impulsive, follow-the-crowd decisions. "Decisions are less divergent and individualized than in earlier times; they are massed. And massed decisions are unrestrained by the inhibitions of self-reliant individuals."[30]

Lynd's individualism must also be qualified by the fact that much of [the consumption by Americans was directly related to both the needs and the luxuries of family life.] Automobiles, radios, and electrical appliances —all of which were leading consumer products of the twenties—were examples of family-based items, though they also may have fulfilled individual needs. Items such as silk stockings, cigarettes, beauty aids, sporting goods, and entertainment expenditures probably reflected the more personal concerns of family members. Expenditures in all of these areas grew tremendously in the postwar decade, but the bulk of the purchases fell within the realm of family living, particularly for middle-class families.

The production and consumption of electricity, for instance, attained amazing proportions during the decade and had an emphatic impact upon family life. Stuart Chase estimated that in 1928 roughly 17.6 million homes were wired for electric current, 15.3 million used electric flat irons, 6.83 million had vacuum cleaners, 5 million had washing machines, 4.54 million had electric toasters, 755,000 had electric refrigerators, 348,000 had ironing machines, and 2.6 million had electric heaters. The numbers seem less impressive when compared with the 27 million homes in the United States. As Chase put it, the supersalesman still had work to do.[31]

Nonetheless, a study done at Mount Holyoke College on the use of electrical appliances in the home indicated that the decade of the twenties marked a great advance in their use for domestic purposes.[32] There were 764 households included in the study, obtained through Mount Holyoke students who were willing to give information regarding their families. In other words, these were middle-class families with above average incomes, as indicated by the fact that they were able to send a daughter to college. All but seven were using some electrical appliances in 1929, and all but five were connected with electrical power. In 1919, a majority of them had either no appliances at all or less than three, but by 1929 over half of them had as many as five or more. When the households were grouped according to the number of appliances used, the largest group in 1919 had none at all, but by 1929 each household in the largest group was using four appliances. In 1919 no household reported as many as a dozen appliances, but in 1929 ten families were using twelve or more.

Because the families of Mount Holyoke students were not representative of the population as a whole, an attempt was made to compare their homes with the homes of the city's wage-earning population. The homes of 201 women who attended the Holyoke Home Informational Center were chosen for this project. The comparison showed that the proportion in each group owning the more common and useful appliances, such as washing machines and electric irons, corresponded very closely. Other items, such as toasters, percolators, and sewing machines, were used by substantial numbers in both groups, although to a much smaller extent by the wage-earning families of the town. Electric ranges and refrigerators, the most expensive items on the list, were used infrequently by the wage-earning families as compared to the higher income group.

These comparisons indicate that by the late 1920s, many electrical appliances for family use were no longer considered luxuries. Even such an expensive item as a washing machine, because of its great labor-saving value, was used by 52 percent of the families in both groups. In other words, the great convenience afforded by these applicances made them common possessions even in the lower income families.

Even more revolutionary than the widespread use of electrical appliances was the emergence of the automobile as a factor that affected both family expenditures and family life. The combination of higher real earnings and technological development gave families an opportunity to allocate a higher proportion of their income to travel and transportation. Related causes were the migration from the central cities to fringe areas, the reduction in the length of the work week which resulted in more leisure time, and perhaps most important, the growth of installment credit to finance the purchase of consumer durable goods, of which the automobile was the most costly item.[33]

Installment buying and the small-loan facilities that developed parallel to the credit system enabled many Americans to change their consumption patterns qualitatively as well as quantitatively. Although they might not spend much more in volume, they were able, by spending a small amount each month, to buy a large, expensive item that had a qualitative impact on their life-style. Also, the fact that credit and loans were available, even to the low-income family, increased the choices of that family in the use of their income. Installment buying was certainly not a new phenomenon in the 1920s, but it rose heavily in volume after 1921, particularly with regard to the automobile. By 1925 three-fourths of all sales of motor vehicles, new and used, were made on time-payment plans. Other items were increasingly purchased on credit, especially major household goods such as refrigerators, washing machines, and radios, as well as jewelry and even European and domestic travel. Credit facilities actually covered only about 10 percent of family expenditures, but small loan facilities provided an increasingly important alternative.[34]

Until the 1920s the automobile was a luxury item reserved for the well-to-do or those few people who used it in their work, such as farmers, doctors, other professionals, and business people. Then the shift to mass production in the second decade of the century resulted in productivity gains and price reductions. Production of cars advanced from 181,000 in 1910 to almost 2 million in 1920, or about one car for every 13 families.[35]

Despite this increase in productivity, only one out of every 18 families of urban workers surveyed by the Department of Labor in 1917-1919 owned an automobile. The cost was still prohibitive for families who were living on an average income of $1,500. However, about 11 percent of the workers whose family income exceeded $1,800 owned cars. Although the next comprehensive study of car ownership among workers was not done until the mid-thirties, there is evidence that the number of cars in America rose rapidly during the 1920s. Car registrations tripled between 1919 and 1929, and in the later year they were equivalent to one car for every 1.3 families. In 1930, in a country with less than 30 million families, more than 23 million passenger cars were registered. Even allowing for the fact that some cars were used primarily for business and some families owned more than one car, these figures show that in all probability nearly two-thirds of the families in the United States owned automobiles by 1930.[36]

The periodicals of the twenties were filled with articles on the automobile, its cost, its maintenance, its varied uses, and its effect on social and family life. As early as 1923 professional economists were concerned that the automobile market had reached the saturation point because only 2 million families made over $2,000 a year—the minimum income necessary to support a car, according to this point of view. Yet by 1929 it had become apparent that many families—perhaps more than one million—owned two cars.[37]

Not everyone greeted the advent of the automobile with enthusiasm. Nostalgia for the preauto days was evident in much of the popular writing, and the auto received a great deal of criticism for its supposed contribution to the disintegration of family life.[38] But others could see the practical advantages of the new "toy" as well, and during the first half of the decade the emphasis was on the automobile as a useful vehicle, one that could save the family time and money. The modern housewife could use the car for shopping, running errands, and taking the children on a ride. City children could be taken to the countryside—an obvious benefit to their health and education. And the car kept the family together for recreation and gave it more freedom in choosing a location for its home.[39]

No matter how much controversy the automobile engendered, it had definitely caught the imagination of the American people at all social and economic levels. Robert and Helen Lynd, in their study of Middletown, reported that at the end of 1923 there were 6,221 cars in the city, one for every 6.1 persons, or roughly two for every three families. Among the business class, at least, ownership of an automobile had become an accepted essential of normal living.[40]

The growing acceptance of the automobile and the value changes that came in its wake not only resulted in a disequilibrium of old ways of doing things but also created disturbing inroads upon the family budget. It was not unusual for a family to mortgage a home in order to buy an automobile, and its purchase and upkeep often cut into potential family savings. Autos were sometimes bought at the expense of other basic items such as food and clothing. It was evident to some observers, even in the early twenties, that many families of moderate means were quite willing to make serious sacrifices in order to possess an automobile.[41]

There is no record of individual expenditures on automobile purchase and maintenance during the twenties, but a number of estimates indicate the relative amount of consumer income that went into automobiles. *Business Week* estimated that 6.2 percent of the total national income in 1919 was spent on automobiles and that the figure was up to 10.7 percent in 1929. Figuring out the expenditure per family was more difficult. Elizabeth E. Hoyt put it at about 5 percent of the family income, and Howard F. Bigelow put it at 6 or 7 percent, but there was no uniformity in either the amount or the percentage of the individual family income spent on a car. Some families had no car, while others had two, but beyond these extremes, expenditure varied according to the type of car owned, the use to which it was put, and the repair and upkeep needed.[42]

The original outlay of capital was the biggest expense. Bigelow found in his study of a small group of families of moderate income that many families were able to operate an automobile on as little as 5 percent of the family expenditures. But in the year that an old model was replaced with a later model, automobile expenditures could amount to 15, 20, 25, or even 30 percent of current expenditures. The family that traded for a new car every year was thus spending a much higher percentage of its income for automobile expense than the family that drove a car for five or six years. But the appeal of a new model was already strong during this decade, and a family gained status as much from the year of its car as from the make.[43]

The automobile had an importance to the American way of life that was symbolic as much as actual, for it represented a new attitude toward family spending. As was true of many of the modern conveniences, the auto was something that the American family could have done without, but nearly all families were willing to sacrifice much for the pleasure, freedom, style, and convenience it offered. In this sense, it was symbolic of a new value system that was to have its impact upon American cultural life in general and upon the family in particular. The automobile stood for the American standard of living which all could aspire to, many would attain, and some would never know.

The term "American standard of living" was used rather freely in the second and third decades of the century—usually without definition. But students of the economy tried to be more precise in their use of the term. E. T. Devine defined it as simply "all those things which one insists upon having."[44] Kyrk described it as "an attitude toward, a way of regarding or of judging, a given mode of life."[45] Perhaps the most complete and straightforward explanation was offered by Bigelow. A standard of living consists "of those goods and services which an individual, a family, or a social group is accustomed to enjoy and which it considers so essential to respectable existence that it is willing to make any reasonable sacrifice to obtain them, such as postponing marriage, limiting the size of the family after marriage, or working longer hours."[46]

A family's standard of living is not the same as its manner, scale, or plane of living. These three terms all refer to the way that the family actually lives. For many twentieth-century families the manner of living is often somewhat below the family's ideal standard. Thus the American family exerts a great deal of time and effort on attaining its standard, only to see that standard move out of reach again.

A study done in 1928 of Yale University faculty members revealed the extent to which standards of living were a source of frustration to all economic levels. The families cooperating in the investigation were asked to give such data as the amount of their salaries and other income and of their principle expenditures as well as a description of their mode of life. The returns were arranged in fifty-four groups, each group containing families of similar size and economic status. The first group, consisting of husband and wife without children and with an income of about $2,000, noted that the level of living possible to them was "life at the cheapest and barest with nothing over for the emergencies of sickness and childbirth." Yet four-fifths of all American families had incomes that did not rise above this level unless supplemented by the earnings of children, and only when the size of the family exceeded five was this income considered inadequate.[47]

Apparently life was no more satisfactory for Yale faculty members at higher levels of income. Those with salaries of $2,500 reported that "a man and his wife must live with extreme frugality." At $3,000 the group in question felt that "for a man and wife it is life on the simplest plane," although probably not even 5 percent of all American families enjoyed this level of income. A faculty family with young children that made $4,000, "must live with extreme economy in the cheapest obtainable apartment." At the $5,000 level they "achieve nothing better than 'hand to mouth living'." At $6,000, "the family containing young children can barely break even," and on $7,000 they "make ends meet only by keeping the expense for service as low as possible." The group with incomes of $8,500 "live on the edge of a deficit." Even at $12,000, if there were school-age children, schooling was said to be limited and life insurance inadequate.

These opinions make evident that standards of living were relative. The families who described their mode of living as unsatisfactory in comparison to their standard of living indicated that they felt restricted in their freedom of choice and their optional consumption by incomes that they deemed inadequate, in spite of the fact that their incomes were far above those of average American families. A study done by Jessica Peixotto in 1927 revealed that the faculty at the University of California, Berkeley, experienced a similar dissatisfaction with their professional standard of living.[48] Yet the subjects of their research were living at a level that most Americans could only envy.

The standard of living that the 96 subjects of Peixotto's study hoped to maintain on their yearly salary was doctor or lawyer's; that is, it was a professional standard of living. It included simple food, with an occasional meal away from home; a house large enough for a family of four, with at least two bedrooms, a study, and quarters for the help; and a household operating fund to cover water, light, fuel, laundry, repairs, upkeep, and some surplus for service. The income was also expected to provide at least 10 percent in savings and money for normal health care. Most significant, the "right to satisfy a modest desire" for books, music, the theater, travel and entertainment of friends was "taken for granted."[49]

The faculty families did not feel that they were being paid enough to achieve this accepted standard, although their salaries ranged from $1,800 to $16,000. The great majority of the salaries—90 percent, in fact —were between $2,000 and $5,000, with only 5 percent of the families getting less than $2,000 and 5 percent getting more than $5,000. Thus, 90 percent of these families were living at the 1923 level of "comfort" for a family of five. And most of the families were small. Only 20 percent had three or more children; more than half had one child or none. The average number of children in a family was 1.5; the average family size was 3.5 persons.

A further indication that these families were living well was that they spent a relatively small proportion of their income on food, yet they ate fairly well. But Engel's laws on consumption and expenditure, developed in the nineteenth century, state that "the poorer the family, the greater the proportion of the total expenditure which must be devoted to the provision of food."[50] Peixotto suggested that an increase in income did not result in increased food expenditure because most of the families placed so little relative value upon this necessary item.[51] But the truth is that there was no reason for them to expand expenses on this item, because they were already eating at a level nearly twice as high as that deemed necessary for adequate subsistence by food specialists. Sixty-five families responded to this part of the questionnaire, with an average household size of 3.9 persons. They spent $.60 per day per capita, in comparison to estimates made by relief budget experts which put the expense of minimum diet requirements at $.36-.39. The University of California families were living quite well as far as the necessities of life were concerned. It was the extras—the miscellaneous items—that made their salaries seem inadequate, at least to themselves. The mean percentage that was spent on miscellaneous items for all 96 families was 43.1 percent. For those making more than $7,000, the mean percentage was over 50 percent. Automobiles consumed a large proportional amount, since 57 percent of the families owned them, and those who did spent as much on them as clothing. Other miscellaneous expenditures that ranked high included investments, health, recreation, and dependents outside the home.[52]

Yet those families spent no more proportionally on miscellaneous items than did the American people as a whole. According to a study done in 1932 by *Business Week*, 48.4 percent of the total national income in 1929 was spent on items other than food, clothing, housing, and home operating expenses, as compared to 36.6 percent in 1919. Not all of these expenditures were of a frivolous nature. Insurance and investments, for example, took 11.8 percent of the national income expenditure, up from 5.2 percent in 1919. Nonetheless, 27.9 percent of the national income was spent on items such as motor cars, smoking, drinking and drugs, jewelry and personal adornment, confectionery and chewing gum, recreation, and other personal expenditures. In 1919, 21.5 percent of the total national income was spent in this manner.[53] The proportion varied greatly according to economic level. Peixotto found that faculty members who made between $2,000 and $3,000 spent only 37.8 percent of their income on miscellaneous items, including insurance, investment, and education, while those making $10,000 and over spent 56 percent of their income in this way.[54]

Inasmuch as the income level of these faculty families was above average for middle-class American families, their mode of living was probably also above average. With respect to the ideal standard of living, these families undoubtedly had some expectations that went beyond those of the average middle-class family in terms of quality. But, Peixotto suggested, the American standard of living, as opposed to the mode or plane of living, was a professional standard, and that all Americans aspired toward the professional life. The professional standard of living was peculiarly American because it was an indication of upward striving and, less obviously, because it placed chief emphasis upon "higher wants."[55]

Peixotto may have overstated the influence of the professional class as a reference group for other classes in society, for values with respect to expenditure varied greatly by class, ethnicity, and other characteristics. But middle-class and lower-class families, like professional families, had a standard of living related not so much to need as to expectation. Expenditures tended to show the influence of a dual attitude toward thrift. On the one hand, thrift was greatly respected, particularly in the purchase of necessities; on the other hand, this respect competed with the approval of spending to satisfy increasing wants. The essential characteristic of the American standard of living, according to Peixotto, "is not belief in abstinence, but rather this exuberant creed that the scale of wants of individuals and families must and should increase in volume, in variety and in intensity; that expanding and varying wants spell increase of personal happiness and general well-being."[56]

Much of the problem of a standard of living, related not so much to need as to expectation. Many families were tempted to live beyond their means and yet, in spite of the wide array of luxury items purchased by their members, still lived below the budget level of health and decency compiled by the United States Department of Labor in 1920. In most cases a low standard of living was forced upon families that simply had a low income, but in other cases consumption choices were made at the expense of the necessities. "It is not a matter of adding luxuries and comforts to an added supply of the prime essentials, but of forcing in luxuries and alleged comforts at the cost of essentials."[57]

[The 1920s represented a whole new era with respect to consumption, standard of living, and the economics of family life.]Americans were accosted with an unprecedented display of material goods, accompanied by a barrage of advertisements inducing them to buy, an increase in real income, and new opportunities for borrowing money to partake of the status and comforts that went with consumption. Add these economic factors to the psychological changes of the twenties, including increased individualization, liberalized social and sexual mores, and growing confidence in the upward curve of the economic cycle, and it is no wonder that so many families were confused by the possibilities open to them and that many of them were simply unable to cope with the problems of budgeting a limited income against unlimited wants.

Although the new trends in consumption played havoc with the family budget, they also contributed to a new interest in family life at a time when the work role was losing its intrinsic value for many people. Consumption may have been a welcome diversion, and no doubt for some workers it was the only thing that made work tolerable at all. As Vance Packard described later decades, "Ever more people . . . find their main life satisfaction in their consumptive role rather than their productive role."[58] Work takes on an instrumental nature, according to the sociologist Harold L. Sheppard, when it "becomes the means by which a man is able to achieve valued goals unrelated to the job. A 'good job' thus is one that allows the maximization of these goals with a minimum of effort and with as good physical conditions as possible."[59]

That a similar sentiment was already a part of economic life in the twenties is reflected in the Lynds' *Middletown*. For most people, both working men and businessmen, the satisfaction which they derived from their jobs was declining. Particularly among the majority of the numerically dominant working-class group, there was a decrease in the psychological satisfactions formerly derived from the sense of craftsmanship and group solidarity. Furthermore, although some working-class people were able to see a better future for their children, they saw no prospect of improving their own job situation: "For both working and business class no other accompaniment of getting a living approaches in importance the money received for their work. It is more this future, instrumental aspect of work, rather than the intrinsic satisfactions involved, that keeps Middletown working so hard as more and more of the activities of living are coming to be strained through the bars of the dollar sign."[60]

The changing values of the 1920s with regard to economic life in America had a two-sided effect on family life. On the one hand, the emphasis on consumption often led to a deteriorated standard of living in terms of necessities for the families that insisted upon luxuries that they could not afford. On the other hand, the availability of consumer goods that could actually improve family life may have had a beneficial effect on family unity. Certainly the man who worked to pay for an automobile, a refrigerator, or a radio was contributing to a family identity, but that identity was maintained through possessions rather than production. In fact, while work life was losing its intrinsic value for some workers, family life, with its new focus on pleasure-giving consumer products, was possibly becoming of more central importance rather than less.

[Consumerism and the modern standard of living gave the term "economic need" a new definition. Instead of merely referring to food, clothing, and shelter, economic need came to mean anything that a particular family was unwilling to go without. And the list of these items expanded greatly during the twenties. One way to gain the desired items was to go into debt; another way was to buy less of the necessities. Still another way was for additional family members to join the work force. Multi-wage-earner families were hardly a new development in the 1920s, for women and children had always made an economic contribution to family life in both rural and urban settings. But during the period 1920-1940 the emphasis turned away from working children and focused instead upon working wives and mothers. Even middle-class wives, who a decade or two earlier would not have considered the possibility of work outside the home, were tentatively accepted, or at least grudgingly tolerated, in certain occupational fields.

When the American dream of prosperity came to an end in 1929, American families at all economic levels were hard hit. For those at the bottom, the Great Depression was an extension and intensification of the hard times they had always suffered. Families who had been marginally independent were pushed across the line into poverty and dependency. But even relatively affluent middle-class families saw their accustomed standard of living come to an effective demise or at least start a shaky decline. In the thirties, it was economic need at all levels that pushed married women into the job market.

2

Deficit Living

The economic complexities of family life became greatly intensified during the 1930s. Family expectations with respect to standard of living remained high, but the means to maintain these expectations declined. There were a variety of ways to meet the crunch. Some families borrowed, while others simply did not pay their bills. Some moved in with relatives, and some went on relief. None of these responses were exclusive of the others, and all of them were particularly characteristic of low income families living on the earnings of marginal workers who experienced frequent unemployment.

[The most logical way for families at all income levels to meet the economic crisis was to cut back on expenditures, but although demand certainly declined, especially between 1929 and 1933, the American people as a whole managed to maintain a remarkably high level of consumption during the Depression.[1] Many families were able to maintain an acceptable standard of living by placing "additional workers" in the labor force. Thus, the economics of family life was an essential ingredient among the several factors that brought married women into the labor force during the thirties, but since women were often the financial managers for their families, it also intensified their roles at home.]

The Great Depression had a varied impact upon American families, not only in terms of intensity but also in terms of time and space. For instance, Midwestern farm families and coal mining families in the Appalachians, along with many others engaged in seasonal work or declining industries, experienced their own personal depression during the early 1920s; in fact, for many families the Depression was just an extreme case of the economic cycle inherent in the American economy. As Grace Abbott pointed out, underemployment and seasonal unemployment had been the general rule among coal miners for three decades prior to 1922. They had come to be regarded as the inevitable result of the modern industrial system. Industry needed a reserve labor supply to meet its peak seasonal demands, but when demand fell off, it dismissed its workers without notice and with no responsibility to them.[2]

The class bias of the more fortunate elements of society made it difficult for them to respond sympathetically to problems of periodical unemployment. This same bias affected their judgment of economic conditions in the first few years after the crash of 1929. The Lynds reported that Middletown was slow to accept the actuality of Depression; the town "did not ship much water in the fall of 1929," and it entered 1930 optimistically. The stock market crash "was not popularly regarded as having much relation to the smooth-running cams of Middletown's factories and the Saturday-night crowds in the downtown shopping section." Retail business was the measure of good times, according to businessmen, and using this standard, they argued that the Depression did not hit Middletown until 1932. But workers had a different perspective, and by 1930 every fourth factory worker in the town had lost his job.[3]

The Depression became a reality at the personal level only when an individual lost his job, suffered a wage cut, or saw his profits go down. But by 1932, everyone was aware of its existence, and most Americans were apprehensive of their economic future. Exposure to the Depression varied across segments of the population, defined by age, sex, occupation, race, and residence. Not all Americans suffered heavy economic losses or unemployment during the thirties. For at least 50 percent of the population, these were not years of great deprivation. But the sense of imminent disaster, the despair and demoralizing fear of losing one's job, home, and dignity, spread through the middle class as well as the more vulnerable masses.[4]

In 1932 the National Industrial Conference Board completed a survey of some 1,500 companies in manufacturing, mining, transportation utilities, and trade. Together these concerns had employed more than two million workers in 1929. By 1932, employment had declined 26 percent; but by the same time executive salaries had been cut 20 percent, routine salaries, 15 percent, and wage rates, 13 percent.[5] Thus unemployment was only a part of the problem. Beyond the debilitating effects of joblessness and the demoralizing aspects of relief, American families had to accept the fact that even if they held on to their jobs, their incomes were shrinking.

The cost of living dropped precipitately during these years, but it could not keep pace with the severe reductions in average income. Wage rates tended to keep in line with the reduction in cost of living, but average income declined more rapidly because workers were working shorter hours. According to the National Industrial Conference Board survey, although wage reductions during 1929-1932 were 13 percent, in comparison to a reduction in cost of living of 20.7 percent, the average hours of work per week were cut 24 percent. Workers were therefore faced with an overall reduction in income of 32 percent. Wage-earners were more often affected by shorter hours than were salaried workers, so although their wage reductions did not appear to be as large, their overall loss of income was greater.[6]

The shrinking income of the average wage-earner and low-salaried worker clashed with the modern expectations of what constituted a decent standard of living. So much attention has been paid to the suffering of the unemployed and the destitute that those who were able to retain their jobs throughout most of the Depression, or those who were temporarily out of work but nonetheless remained independent of welfare agencies, are often overlooked.[7] Although these families did not suffer to the extent of families on relief or of those, both urban and rural, who eked out a bare existence without public relief, they nonetheless felt their deprivation keenly. These were the families who, although nervous about their job security, were also concerned about their shrinking income. But because they had an income to manipulate, they were more easily able to emerge from the Depression with family intact and values nearly so.

Nonrelief families ranged from those in borderline poverty, at one extreme, to the obviously wealthy at the other extreme. When projects were established to aid families on relief, it was often found that their neighbors were equally in need. A school lunch project, set up in Utah in 1935, was intended to serve only grade school children of families on relief. But the sponsors soon recognized that the children of nonrelief families were also hungry and that the high school girls and boys needed nourishing food as much as the younger children. Similarly, a survey in Colorado revealed that 50 percent of all children attending school in the state were receiving insufficient food and that almost as many were dangerously undernourished. In some communities 80 percent of the children were 15 percent underweight. As a result, county-wide school lunch projects were established under the Works Progress Administration (WPA) with the cooperation of parent-teacher associations and civic groups.[8]

Surveys of this type offer convincing evidence that many families in all categories were unable to establish a healthful standard of living. Often nonrelief families used the free medical and nursing services of large cities. Lilian Brandt observed that in the winter of 1930-1931 the Health Department Services of New York City reached a new strata of the population, what she called the "new poor." The visiting-nurse organizations gave free services to families who normally would have engaged a private nurse or even a private room in a hospital. Likewise, many of the applicants at family relief agencies came from distinctly higher economic levels and had contributed to these same agencies in better years.[9]

Relief statistics could not reveal the intensity of economic distress or even the full extent of unemployment. In the winter of 1930-1931, less than half of the unemployed of Philadelphia were aided by unemployment relief projects, which meant that the others must have been living on the verge of destitution. In spite of the fact that not only relief assistance but also other resources such as emergency work and noninterest-bearing loans were available, most families preferred to get along without public assistance.[10]

There were a number of ways that families could adapt to unemployment or reduced wages. The first barrier against disaster was the kinship system. A number of statistical studies done during the 1930s indicated that during a period of unemployment there was a tendency for families to combine. A survey of workers who had been laid off by the United States Rubber Company in two different communities—Hartford and New Haven, Connecticut—revealed that in each community, 15 percent of the unemployed families included various relatives in addition to the husband, wife, and children. The outsiders were not always completely dependent. Occasionally they were regular wage-earners whose income was decisive in holding the family together. In the case of elderly relatives, they often had a little property or income which supplemented family income. As the survey described the situation: "Whole families combine in a sort of superfamily, so that one rent payment will do instead of two. Relatives of all degrees gather round an income like flies around honey—anyone who has a job and an income will find himself swamped either with appeals for help or with nonpaying guests."[11]

If relatives did not move in together, the help received from those who were better off was usually in the form of loans, gifts of clothing, or an occasional free meal. Unfortunately, however, if one branch of a family was visited by hard times, it was unlikely that another branch would escape unscathed. Thus, helping family members could mean a considerable sacrifice for the wage-earner.

An example of a helping relationship was that which existed between two Detroit families in which the wives were sisters. In 1935 Gerald Corkum, the husband of one sister, had an income of about $1,200 a year as an automobile worker. Although he had been unemployed for about a year in the depths of the Depression, he had never been on relief, and he regained his job. The Corkums were making mortgage payments on a five-room house; they had been married twelve years and had no children. Through careful budgeting and occasional part-time work on the part of the wife, this couple was able to survive the Depression quite comfortably.

Their relatives, the Dales, were less fortunate. They had been on and off relief for two years. They had two little girls, four and six years old, and the wife had had an operation for cancer. Their relief allotment of $9.60 every two weeks seldom carried them through. Toward the end of each relief check they ate their meals with the Corkums, and sometimes Mrs. Dale and her two children would stay for several days until the next relief check was due. On Sundays the Corkums put together a picnic dinner and took the Dales to a picnic area or public beach were the children could play.[12] Like so many families during the Depression, the Corkums were not able to give direct financial aid to their relatives, but the kinship tie was a strong one, and the help that was provided must have had psychological as well as material benefit.

The extent of material aid on the part of relatives was considerable. Webster Powell, who surveyed 1,439 applicants at the Emergency Work Bureau in Philadelphia, found that 185, or 12.9 percent, of the applicants received help from friends or relatives in the form of meals and gifts, not including loans; and that 144, or 10 percent, lived with friends or relatives. Although these figures represent a substantial proportion of all families, it is also evident that help from friends and family was not as important as several other methods of getting along. The first line of recourse was savings: 53.5 percent had at least some savings upon which to fall back. The next step was to go into debt: over 50 percent delayed paying the landlord; 26 percent borrowed money from banks, loan companies, or friends and relatives; and 19 percent obtained credit from their grocers.[13]

The Depression had a twofold effect upon kinship ties. The immediate effect was to restore the ties between families, particularly in the early years of the Depression. Relief policies probably increased this tendency, since families were often forced to get help from relatives before relief was granted to them. But although the Depression accentuated the protective functions of the family, it also provided the stimulus for the passage of protective legislation, which had the long-term effect of enlarging state functions at the expense of family functions.[14]

One way for a family to adapt to Depression conditions was to adopt a lower standard of living. This remedy was accepted with varying degrees of success by nearly all classes in America except the well-to-do. The extent to which families were successful depended upon several factors, some of which they could control and others they could not. These included the cost of living, the family income, the family's material needs and expectations, and the budgeting skill of the family's consumer manager, namely the woman.

The decline in the cost of living between the crash of 1929 and April 1933 was the most hopeful aspect of the Depression for families who had a steady wage-earner (Appendix A). Combined money income in 1931 was approximately 30 percent less than that of 1929, but the cost of living for a workingman's family declined about 15 percent during the same period. Although this was not equal to the decline in money income, the necessities of life—food and clothing—showed the most striking decreases. Food was down 20 percent; clothing, 10 percent. Housing furnishings were also down 10 percent. Other items showed a less impressive decline; rents went down 8 percent, fuel and light, 5 percent, and miscellaneous items declined hardly at all.[15]

The Depression had bottomed out by April 1933, and the cost of living began gradually to rise again. In 1934 it averaged 6 percent higher than in 1933, and in 1935 it rose another 5 percent. By July 1936, it had increased a full 20 percent over the low point in 1933. Food was the chief inflater of living costs during the middle thirties. The combination of crop curtailments by the Agricultural Adjustment Act and droughts shortened the supply of food, and the gradual decrease in unemployment improved the purchasing power of the wage-earner and increased demand. By mid-1937, food was up 41 percent, clothing up 22 percent, and rents were up 31 percent over their low point of January 1934. Fuel and light did not increase; in fact, gas and electricity became slightly cheaper. Miscellaneous items were up 6 percent.[16]

The rise in the cost of living hit white-collar workers on a fixed income particularly hard because they did not experience the same increase in weekly earnings over the years 1933-1936 as did wage-earners. Schoolteachers represented one salaried group whose fortunes varied inversely with those of wage-earners. During the early years of the Depression, teachers' salaries rose while wage-earners suffered a significant decline. But when the real income of wage-earners began to increase, from 1932 to 1934, the real income of teachers was cut by 30 percent.[17]

But wage-earners, as a result of both unemployment and wage reductions, suffered a much greater loss in purchasing power between 1929 and 1932 than white-collar workers. The loss was unequally divided. Those who remained employed throughout the period lost, on the average, only 20 percent of their former purchasing power. But few wage-earners remained employed for the whole period of 1929-1932, just as few were totally unemployed during the period. On the average, the purchasing power of wage-earners in 1932 was 49.5 percent of what it had been in 1929; that of salaried workers was 73.7 percent of the 1929 level. Other classes also fared better than wage-earners. Those who received their income from dividends, interest, rent, royalties, and entrepreneurial endeavors had a purchasing power in 1932 that ranged from 54 percent to 120 percent of the 1929 level.[18]

But gross figures had little meaning to the millions of individual families who had to maintain their standard of living on a limited income. There is evidence that individual family incomes declined sharply during the Depression. Hildegarde Kneeland estimated the distribution of consumer incomes in 1935-1936, using data from a nationwide sample of some 300,000 families. The data showed the net income of the different family members, from profits, dividends, interest, and rent, from pensions, annuities, and benefits, from gifts used for current living expenses, from the occupancy of owned homes, from home-grown food and other home-made products used by the family.[19] Kneeland projected these data to estimate the income distribution of the 39,458,300 "consumer units" in the United States. These consumer units included 29,400,300 families of all sizes and 10,058,000 unattached individuals. The median income of families and individuals combined was $1,070. The median income of families alone was $1,160; that of single adult individuals who were not necessarily employed was $830 (Table 2.1).[20]

A comparison of the 1935-1936 income levels with those of 1929 illustrates the income decline of individual American families. In the years between 1929 and 1936, current-dollar incomes dropped drastically (Table 2.2). But the decline must be qualified, for two reasons. First of all, there was a concomitant decline in the cost of living. Also, the 1929 data are not as reliable as the later figures. Unlike 1935-1936, there was no nationwide sample field survey of family incomes in 1929. Instead, the Brookings Institution constructed a 1929 distribution for families and unattached individuals by combining a variety of different sets of income statistics for persons and then converting them to a family-unit basis. Therefore, the 1929 distribution is roughly estimated, and it is particularly unreliable for the lower end of the income scale.[21] A better perspective on the value of incomes is gained by comparing the mid-years of

Table 2.1   Distribution of family income, 1935-1936

Income level ($)	No. families (1,000s)	% at each level	Cumulative (%)
Under 250	1,163	4.0	4.0
250-500	3,015	10.3	14.2
500-750	3,799	12.9	27.1
750-1,000	4,277	14.6	41.6
1,000-1,250	3,882	13.2	54.9
1,250-1,500	2,865	9.8	64.6
1,500-1,750	2,343	7.8	72.6
1,750-2,000	1,897	6.4	79.0
2,000-2,250	1,421	4.8	83.9
2,250-2,500	1,044	3.6	87.3
2,500-3,000	1,314	4.5	91.9
3,000-3,500	744	2.5	94.4
3,500-4,000	438	1.5	95.9
4,000-4,500	250	.9	96.8
4,500-5,000	153	.5	97.3
Over 5,000	793	2.7	100.0
Total	29,400	100.0	

Source: "Incomes of Families and Single Persons, 1935-1936," *Monthly Labor Review* 47 (October 1938): 730.

Table 2.2   Distribution of family income, 1929 and 1935-1936

Income Level ($)	1929 (%)	1935-36 (%)
Under 500	8.1	14.2
Under 1,000	21.5	41.7
Under 1,500	42.4	64.6
Under 2,000	59.5	79.1
Under 2,500	71.2	87.4
Over 2,500	28.8	12.6

Source: Tables 1.1 and 2.1.

the Depression to the more affluent years of 1929, 1941, and 1944 in terms of 1950 dollars (Table 2.3).

The 1935-1936 figures included many families living on relief, as well as farm families with little or no monetary income. Nonmoney income was estimated, however. For all groups of families this included the net value of the occupancy of an owned home, as well as the estimated value of direct relief received in kind. For farm and village families, it also included the net imputed value of food produced at home for the family's own use and certain other farm-produced goods used by the family.[22]

In spite of the inclusion of imputed income, the distribution of income varied considerably by urban-rural location and occupational class. The inclusion of the 4.5 million families who were receiving relief in 1935-1936 would have increased the proportion in the lower income levels and lowered the average income per family. However, it would not have greatly altered the relative position of the different types of communities. Except in the case of farm families, the proportion of families receiving relief at some time during the year 1935-1936 showed little variation with size of community. The highest proportion was found in rural nonfarm areas, where 19 percent of all families received some relief; the lowest proportion was found in farm areas, which averaged 9 percent of the families on relief. The next lowest proportion was in metropolises of

Table 2.3. Distribution of income among families and unattached individuals, 1929-1944

Income Level (1950$)	1929 (%)	1936 (%)	1941 (%)	1944 (%)
Under 1,000	15.9	19.5	15.1	7.3
1,000-1,999	25.6	29.2	19.9	13.7
2,000-2,999	25.7	20.7	18.5	15.5
3,000-3,999	12.2	12.3	15.7	17.6
4,000-4,999	7.2	7.3	12.3	14.7
Over 5,000	13.4	11.0	18.5	31.2

Source: Selma F. Goldsmith, "The Relation of Census Income Distribution Statistics to Other Income Data," in Conference on Research in Income and Wealth, *An Appraisal of the 1950 Census Data* (Princeton: National Bureau of Economic Research, Princeton University Press, 1958), p. 93; Selma F. Goldsmith *et al.*, "Size Distribution of Income Since the Mid-Thirties," *Review of Economics and Statistics* 36 (February 1954): 4.

1,500,000 population and over, where about 15 percent received relief.[23] In spite of the small proportion of farm families receiving relief, farm families had much smaller incomes than families in other areas, even with the inclusion of nonmoney income. Either the nonmoney income of farmers was greatly underestimated, or the farmers were simply existing at a much lower plane of living than their contemporaries.

Occupational differences in the distribution of income were even more significant than type-of-community difference. In the 1935-1936 sample, occupational group was determined by the occupation from which the largest proportion of all family earnings was derived. Families that had received relief were excluded, resulting in an unusually low proportion of families in the wage-earner group because of the relatively high incidence of relief among families in this category.

Although wage-earners were underrepresented, they still made up 38 percent of all of the nonrelief families. Farm families were another 25 percent. But these two groups had the lowest median incomes—$1,175 and $965, respectively—and were most heavily represented in the lower income ranges. More than 85 percent of all farm families were below $2,000, and more than half were below $1,000. The wage-earning families were also concentrated below $2,000, with only 15 percent above that level. Many of the wage-earner incomes included the earnings of several members of the families, not all of whom were employed in a wage-earning occupation.[24]

Classes that were still doing fairly well, in spite of the Depression, included clerical classes, salaried business classes, and professionals, particularly independent professionals. But altogether these groups made up only about 20 percent of the total.

There was a remarkably unequal distribution of income among occupational groups. For instance, although over half of all independent professionals in 1935-1936 were earning more than $3,000 a year, this was a tiny group of less than 200,000 families, or about 4 percent of the number of families who were receiving relief payments in that year.[25] Thus, the upper income groups must be kept in proper perspective in comparing them to American families as a whole, since they represented only a tiny minority.

Despite mitigating factors such as these occupational differentials and a lowered cost of living, there is no question that the average American family, struggling to make ends meet during the Depression, had a smaller income to work with than at any time during the post-World War I period. Yet this reduction in income did not affect the expenditure patterns and consumption habits of the American people in the expected way.

Perhaps the most surprising thing about the economics of family life during the Depression was the degree to which the American people were able to maintain a fairly high level of consumption, and the degree to which they were unwilling to sacrifice material goods that in earlier decades would have been considered luxuries. A new definition of economic need had emerged during the previous decades of prosperity, and the Depression tested that definition. Even in the face of unemployment, wage reductions, and general economic insecurity, the American people clung to certain material goods and life-styles that had become important elements in the new definition of economic need.

During the years of rising prosperity from 1922 to 1929, the volume production of consumer goods as a whole had gone up 31 percent. But the volume of food production had increased only 13 percent, while that of durable consumption goods, such as houses, automobiles, luggage, and silverware, had risen 53 percent. Thus, in a time of prosperity, Americans were spending their money on items that they were less likely to buy during hard times. When the Depression came, they decreased consumption somewhat, but more important, they changed their patterns of consumption. The purchase of radios and automobiles declined, but the consumption of gasoline went down very little, indicating that although people were forgoing the luxury of a new car, they were hanging on to the old one—and using it. In contrast, telephones were sacrificed rather easily. In 1928 there were 15.9 million telephones in use. By 1930 this figure was up to 17.2 million; but by 1931 it had dropped to 15.1 million.[26]

Because of the falling prices, much less money was spent on physical necessities, such as food and clothing, but the actual quantities consumed declined very little. However, within these two categories there were shifts from one product to another. The quantity of furniture and furnishings purchased from 1928 to 1932 fell comparatively little, and the consumption of notions, toilet articles, books and magazines, toys, and even candy either increased or at least did not decrease during these years. Cigarette consumption fell off only slightly.[27]

A Bureau of Labor Statistics study of consumer purchases in 1935-1936 provided facts on the consumption patterns of families not on relief and at different income levels, using a random sample of about 336,000 families and a smaller sample of about 53,000 families. This study pointed out that changes in family expenditures since World War I had occurred during the 1920s, not the 1930s, and that these changes had had a profound effect upon consumption habits in the thirties, in spite of the decline in income. Faith Williams, director of the study, observed that most families of wage-earners and clerical workers had a higher standard of living in 1935-1936 than similar families had maintained in the postwar years of 1917-1919: "Their diets more nearly approach the recommendation of specialists in human nutrition; they have homes with better lighting; many of them are able to travel more because they have automobiles. The change in the ideas of these workers as to how they ought to live has resulted in fundamental changes in their expenditure pattern."[28]

American families maintained their standard of living, in part by operating at a loss. In 16 out of 35 cities for which figures were available, the entire group studied at the income level of $1,200 to $1,500 showed a net deficit for the year. In all but two of the nineteen cities where net savings were recorded, the average amount saved in 1935-1936 was smaller than that shown by the group studied in earlier years. Thus, although the American people held to a high standard of living, they were often having difficulty supporting their consumption habits on the incomes that they earned.

The problem of living within one's income varied from city to city. New York was the most expensive place to live: 17 out of every 100 New York families with yearly earnings have $10,000 could not, or would not, live within their income. In Chicago, five persons out of every 100 earning from $5,000 to $7,500 operated at a loss, and one out of every 100 in this group just broke even. Families in the medium-sized cities of the West Central region had an easier time of it. On the average, they managed to put aside $1.00 a year on an income of $1,000 to $1,250. In other words, they were just breaking even. In comparably-sized cities of New England the average family could not come out ahead unless it had an income above $2,000.[29]

The study of consumer purchases not only is a valuable assessment of actual expenditures but also provides a means of determining the value placed upon particular consumer items at the different income levels. The families studied in 1934-1936 with respect to expenditures were carefully selected to represent a cross-section of all families of employed white wage-earners and low-salaried clerical workers in selected cities. Since the information was being obtained primarily for the purpose of providing a basis for indexes of living costs, it was felt that it should not reflect the distorted spending of families whose incomes had been abnormally low or irregular. For that reason, no data were included from families whose incomes were under $500 a year or from families who received relief during the year. Unfortunately, this exclusion of blacks, families on relief, and very low-income families created a bias in favor of relative affluence. The nature of this bias should be kept in mind when considering the following expenditure patterns.

Consumer expenditures were divided into several main categories—food, clothing, housing, furnishing and equipment, and "all other items." A comparison of expenditures in these categories with data from a study of income and expenditure in 1917-1919 reveals that the American people made significant changes in their patterns of consumption during the fifteen-year interval. As Williams observed, "an important change in attitudes toward consumption expenditures had occurred among moderate-income urban families in the interval between the two investigations."[30]

Williams used families at the income level of $1,200 to $1,500 as a representative group to show the postwar changes in each of the cities investigated. Adjustments were made to reflect the price realignments which occurred during the interval between the two studies. The purchasing power of the worker's dollar was on the average slightly higher in 1934-1936 than it had been in 1917-1919. Food prices were consistently lower by as much as 16 percent to 38 percent in each of the cities covered by both studies. Clothing prices were also lower by 5 percent to 31 percent. The differences in the price of rent, fuel, and light varied greatly from city to city. Furnishings and household equipment were generally lower in the later period, but miscellaneous items were higher in every city. The Bureau of Labor Statistics eliminated these price differences by applying the cost of items in the 1934-1936 period to the average expenditures of the families studied in 1917-1919.

The basic change in expenditure at all income levels was a shift away from essential items—food, clothing, and shelter—toward the miscellaneous items that signify an overall higher standard of living. The pattern of change was very similar in each city. For instance, in twenty-four out of thirty-five cities, average expenditures for food were lower in the later period. This was because food prices were lower, enabling families to eat as well or better on less money. The average amount spent for clothing was down for each city, but expenditures for housing, which included fuel, light, and refrigeration, were higher in every city except one. A large proportion of the 1934-1936 families had electric lighting and modern plumbing, which accounted for the higher costs. Expenditures for furniture and furnishings varied from city to city. Finally, two-thirds of the cities showed a higher average expenditure on miscellaneous items, which included all other expenses.

In spite of the fact that Americans were spending a smaller proportion of their income on food in 1934-1936, they were nonetheless spending more than enough to buy the quantity and quality of food purchased in 1917-1919. In the years after World War I, new developments in agricultural production and in transcontinental refrigerator cars brought fresh fruits and vegetables to urban markets the year round at prices considerably lower than those prevailing before the war. Also, during these years the results of extensive research into the physiological needs of the human body had been popularized to the extent that many Americans were becoming aware of the importance of human nutrition. Consequently there was a larger per capita consumption of milk, oranges, lettuce, spinach, and canned tomatoes in 1934-1936 than in the earlier period. Tomato juice and grapefruit were also consumed in large quantities, whereas they had been almost unknown in 1917-1919. The nutritional value of these foods enhanced the diet of those families able to afford them and thus increased their standard of living.

Not surprisingly, the type of food consumed varied at the different economic levels. The higher income groups tended to buy more fresh fruits and vegetables, as well as more meat and eggs. At the lower levels the market basket was more likely to contain bread, flour and meal, and white or sweet potatoes. In general, as the family's economic well-being improved, it spent a smaller proportion of its income on food, but the actual number of dollars spent was greater than that of low-income families, making it possible to purchase the more expensive items.[31]

Second only to the expense of feeding a family was that of maintaining a home. Average expenditure on housing, which included fuel, light, refrigeration, and the cost of lodging family members away from home, as at college or boarding school, ranged from 22 percent to 38 percent of a family's income, depending on income level, regional location, and size of city. Thus families living in the Northeast paid more for their housing than those in the Southeast or Far West. This was a reflection not only of higher rents but also of the difference in types of dwellings and in heating equipment and costs. Residents of large cities spent more for their housing than did families in middle-sized and small cities at comparable income levels. As family income rose, the amount spent on housing also rose, but at a slower rate. Thus, at the higher income levels, a lower proportion of the family budget was devoted to housing.[32]

Few families were willing to sacrifice good housing, even in the depths of the Depression. Some were forced to make this sacrifice, but not before every alternative had been tried. Clothing, in contrast, was an item that could be sharply contracted or expanded in any given year to meet the particular circumstances of the family. The consumption of clothing in the 1930s declined absolutely as well as proportionately. The lower expenditures can be attributed in part to lower prices, but even if the prices of the 1917-1919 period are equalized with those of 1934-1936, less was spent in the later period. Americans were simply buying fewer clothes.[33] Clothes were relatively durable. They could be handed down, made over, or mended. They represented an item that Depression families were willing to go without.

But other goods were not so easy to give up. The Lynds, in their study of Middletown during the thirties, called the automobile one of the most Depression-proof elements of the family budget, and this was probably true to a greater or lesser degree in all parts of America. The working class, in particular, clung to the automobile as a symbol of their own status and advancement, according to the Lynds: "Car ownership stands to them for a large share of the 'American dream'; they cling to its as they cling to self-respect, and it was not unusual to see a family drive up to the relief commissary in 1935 to stand in line for its four-or-five dollar weekly food dole."[34]

The Lynds were revealing their own class bias in remarking on the working-class emotional dependency on the automobile, for the appeal of this particular mode of transportation was almost universal, and certainly the working class had as much practical need for mobility as the upper classes. In any case, although the number of new cars purchased declined considerably during the early years of the Depression, car registration showed little overall decline between 1929 and 1935. It fell about 10 percent below the 1929 level in 1933, but by 1935 it was only about 2 percent lower than in 1929 and over 4 percent higher than in 1928. The number of car registrations per 1,000 population in Middletown's county went from 173 in 1925 to 192 in 1929, down to 179 in 1930, and up to 215 in 1935.[35]

The residents of Middletown were willing to drive their old car as the Depression wore on, but "they manifestly continued to ride." Although the purchase of new cars was nearly halved between 1929 and 1930, there was a drop of only 4 percent in the dollar volume of gasoline sales between 1929 and 1933.[36] The same tendency was shown on a national scale in a study done for the Social Science Research Council in 1937 on the number of automobiles sold in comparison to the quantity of gasoline sold (Table 2.4). By the 1930s, although a new car was not a necessity for most American families, the use of some kind of automobile was becoming essential.

Table 2.4. Passenger automobiles and gasoline sold, 1929-1936 (1929 base =
100)

Year	Automobiles	Gasoline (gals.)
1929	100	100
1930	62	101
1931	42	104
1932	30	100
1933	30	100
1934	39	104
1935	60	113
1936	69	112

Source: Roland S. Vaile, Research Memorandum on Social Aspects of Consumption in the Depression, Bulletin no. 35 (New York: Social Science Research Council, 1937), p. 19.

By the mid-1930s, expenditures for transportation of all types were about twice as important, relevant to expenditures for all consumer goods and services, as they had been in 1917-1919. But most of the increase was due to the automobile rather than to public conveyances used either for local transportation or for long-distance travel. Families in the income range of $900 to $1,200, spent from 5 to 6 percent of their incomes on transportation, compared to 1 or 2 percent in 1917-1919. Those earning from $1,200 to $2,000, spent 6 to 9 percent of their income on transportation, as compared to 2 or 3 percent in the earlier period for comparable income levels. Automobile ownership was almost universal among families with incomes of $5,000 or more, but it was also fairly common among lower income families. At least one in five of the white nonrelief families with incomes as low as $750 to $1,000 in all of the communities that were studied, except New York and Chicago, reported car ownership during the year 1935-1936. At successive income levels from $1,000 to $5,000, the proportion of families who owned cars increased steadily. For instance, in the income level of $1,250 to $1,500, 40 percent to 75 percent reported car ownership, depending upon the size of the city and the region.[37]

Family size and composition also affected car ownership. A family of two to four members was more likely to own a car than a family of seven or eight, probably for the simple reason that they were better able to afford it. A family with children under sixteen was more likely to own a car than a family of several adult members. Perhaps the presence of children made a car seem more necessary for transportation. There were also regional differences in car ownership. The Rocky Mountain and Pacific Northwest areas had a higher proportion of car owners at all income levels except the highest level. In the largest cities, car operation tended to be more expensive, because of higher garage and parking charges, but was less necessary, since public transportation systems were better developed than in smaller cities. Finally, white families were more likely to own automobiles than black families, even at the same income levels.[38]

The automobile exemplified the fact that it was becoming difficult to draw the line between necessities and luxuries, even in a time of Depression. To many families a radio, the latest movie, a package of cigarettes, or the daily newspaper were as necessary to the family well-being as food, clothing, and shelter. Other items were also questionable. How would one categorize a Boy Scout uniform, for instance? Was it clothing or recreation? Did a vacation trip constitute transportation or recreation? For families at the upper income levels and for those at the bottom it was never an issue to resolve, but for the middle- and lower-middle income families, choices had to be made. Often they were made in favor of items that would have been considered luxuries in the immediate postwar years. Thus, an individual family's definition of economic need had an important bearing upon family living standards and how they were maintained.

Most of the items that offered the possibility of choice could be lumped under the general category of "miscellaneous," which covered a wide range of expenditures, including tobacco (which was the most important miscellaneous item for all income groups except those over $3,500), church contributions, movies, newspapers, games and sports, community chest and welfare, magazines, club dues, and books (which ranked lowest of all these items). In comparing the 1917-1919 period with the mid-thirties, Williams lumped everything beyond food, clothing, housing, and furnishing and equipment, into a category called "all other items." This included transportation, travel, education, cosmetics, haircuts, and all other goods and services affecting personal appearance except clothing. In two-thirds of the cities that were studied, expenditures for these items were higher in 1934-1936 than they would have been if the expenditure patterns of 1917-1919 had been maintained.[39]

The purchase of miscellaneous items increased both absolutely and proportionately as income rose. Thus families earning $500 to $749 annually spent about 6 percent of their income on contributions, recreation, reading, tobacco, and education combined. Those who earned $1,500 to $2,000 spent about 8 percent to 9 percent of this category, and those earning over $5,000 might have spent anywhere from 16 percent to over 20 percent. For those at the lower income levels, this expenditure was less than $50 a year, but for those making over $5,000, it could range anywhere from $700 to well over $2,000. Since nearly 80 percent of all families earned under $2,000, most of them were spending less than $200 a year on this category of expenditures. The 65 percent who were earning less than $1,500 had not much more than $100 a year to spend in this manner.[40]

There still were areas in which American families were not spending enough to meet their needs. Only a few families with relatively high incomes spent enough to provide adequate medical care in 1935-1936. The Bureau of Labor Statistics estimated the cost of adequate care at that time, according to minimum fees, at an average of $75.50 per person per year. Although this was to include everything—long-term illness, dental care, and hospitalization—it may have been an urealistically high estimate. The data obtained in the study of consumer purchases showed that the per person expenditures of large-city families in the median income group actually averaged from $13 to $25 a year. Only a very small proportion of families received clinic service.[41]

Medical care was apparently a low priority item among most families. It was something that could be postponed or limited. Also, it is possible that in small towns and rural areas, certain kinds of medical care were taken for granted by families unable to pay for the service in cash. For instance, the rural doctor might deliver a baby, perform an appendectomy, or give some other service vital to the health of his neighbors; he might be paid in kind or through barter, or he might not be paid at all. But he was probably not in a position to deny the service.[42]

Nonetheless, it is hard to avoid the conclusion that families were stinting on their medical needs. Even without the occasional illnesses that strike on an irregular basis, the inclusion of dental care and physical examinations should have resulted in at least some expenditures for all families in any given year. But many families even in the middle and upper portion of the income scale had no expenditures during an entire year. Medical care expenditures were illustrative of what many economists felt was poor judgment on the part of family consumers. Day Monroe, a home economist, argued that even families with very low incomes could improve their standard of living somewhat by improving their buying habits. Better choices of food, for instance, could result in adequate diets without increasing expenditures, and the same general principle held true for other items.[43]

No doubt more intelligent buying habits could have resulted in a higher standard of living for some families. The problem was partly one of education, but it was more importantly a matter of changing values. As American families of all income levels raised their expectations, the expenditure pattern of the individual family was dependent upon personal values rather than the sophisticated opinions of economists and social workers.

Many families, especially those in the middle to upper income groups, made a conscious effort to plan their expenditures in response to wage reductions or changes in employment. Women's magazines and popular journals had special sections on budgeting, and even ran contests for readers who wished to devise and send in the perfect budget. That this was definitely an upper-middle class phenomenon is indicated by the incomes that the participating families had to budget—the lowest was $1,200, and they ranged to $3,000 and even $5,000. But the ways in which these incomes were handled gives a good indication of the middle-class values that were largely sustained even during the country's deepest and longest depression.

Most of the women (and it was always women) who wrote personal accounts of their budgeting experience to the journals did so in a light-hearted manner. Obviously there was something fun about returning to the "plain living" of grandma's day, especially when that plain living was sustained on a $2,500 a year salary. One woman, who claimed that her family was of "moderate means," reported her beauty operator's definition of life's necessities: "In these days a permanent wave is as essential as a radio or a good bootlegger."[44]

Although the writer recoiled from this outline of life's needs, she probably possessed at least the radio, if not the bootlegger. Her Depression budget reduced the family to cheaper rent, home-baked goods, no servants, and public school for the children. The sacrifices were primarily psychological, because the family had so many of the "extras" that cutting back entailed little actual suffering. In fact, it was seen by the family as merely a healthful and virtuous return to the plain living of previous generations. Nonetheless, although this family did not slip below the level of comfort, there were psychological problems to be faced: "learning is more difficult at forty than it was at eight. Indeed, to us elders the march backwards entails many things that leave a bitter taste. In youth poverty is a novitiate, a preparation for the race; in middle life one is a little terrified by the thought that it is the taking of final vows, that the race has been run."[45]

A similar middle- to upper-middle-class bias was expressed by four women who wrote letters to *Ladies' Home Journal*, describing how they managed to exist on $2,500 a year—an income that put them among the top 29 percent in the nation as of 1929 and the top 12 percent as of 1935-1936. Once again, these individuals self-righteously did their own sewing, attended free programs at the university, turned off lights, ate apples instead of candy, and practiced home canning. But they were able to engage in economies on items that less well-to-do families would have had to forgo altogether. For instance, buying in quantity was a frequently mentioned economy measure that would have hardly been feasible at low income levels. Also, "good quality" was a necessary prerequisite in the purchase of many items, including clothing, mechanical and electrical appliances, and food. One mother, who pointed out that raising five small children on $2,500 a year was "a serious struggle" requiring "prayer and push," did not stint on household operating expenses: "Good equipment makes a good worker a better worker. No work is done outside of the home, but I have an electric sweeper, washer, and refrigerator. I found electric refrigeration enough cheaper than the older method to enable one to buy an electric refrigerator on the monthly payment plan. Even my kitchen broom and paring knife have quality."[46]

The women who sustained their families on these incomes, which they considered moderate, had difficulty understanding their more careless and less fortunate contemporaries. Even those in similar economic circumstances were often the target of their reproach. A faculty wife, whose husband earned about $3,000 in 1936, complained that Americans were unwilling to forgo material pleasures. Her acquaintances on the faculty were perpetually broke and continually "crabbing" about the Depression, but she noted that they had never been able to live on their incomes even before reductions. Although she denied that she was trying to belittle the Depression, she felt that many of its tragedies were the result of the softness that prosperity had fostered.[47]

Not all middle-class families survived the Depression as comfortably as these fortunate few. For many there were genuine sacrifices to be made and difficult tasks to accomplish. The wife of a white-collar worker admitted that "unaccustomed poverty tries both soul and body." The extra work, which fell primarily upon the wife and mother, included more careful shopping, more darning and mending, and the ability to make do with makeshift items. But the extra work was only a part of thrift; it also included sitting in a damp chilly house during the first cold days of autumn in order to conserve coal, denying the children simple pleasures, and watching a saddened, gray, and silent husband return "fear-haunted" to his office job every day.[48] The families of white-collar workers may not have been starving, but they were frightened, and the Depression was a very real thing in their lives.

Sometimes the "fear-haunted" husband had no job to which he could return. Unemployment was more common at the lower income levels, but professional and business classes were not immune. A man who was employed in the foreign service department of a large public utility company was released from his job in 1929. His family had been accustomed to a high standard of living, which included six months out of every year overseas, meeting and entertaining the "right people." Before their struggle with the Depression was over, they had experienced malnutrition, relief, and the social and psychological problems related to these conditions. But they emerged from their ordeal in remarkably good form, owing to the strength and spirit of the woman, the adaptability of the children, and the determination of the father, who willingly accepted a work relief job that he at one time would have considered beneath him. Eventually he found a regular job and was able to re-establish himself. This was an example of one family who, for public consumption at least, was not embittered by its Depression experience but rather felt that it had benefited through adversity.[49]

In general, most of the accounts of budgeting written during the 1930s pertained either to the relief family living on a minimum standard budget or to the upper-middle-class family living on a comfortable income.[50] There were some exceptions to this tendency. In 1931, *Literary Digest* ran an article called "Champion Nickel-Stretchers" which described the standard of living of three different families: a family of four living on $1,800; a family of seventeen, fifteen of them children, living on the same amount; and a black family with three children, living on $1,040 a year. The first of these, the Pennypackers, spent half of their income on house payments, taxes, and insurance. Aside from their house, nothing was bought on time; everything was cash. Mrs. Pennypacker made almost all the clothing. In particular, she prided herself on her "penny-pinching" menus, which she called the most adjustable in the world.[51]

Actually, the Pennypackers should have had no problem living on their income. At $1,800 they were in the upper quarter of the income range and had the added advantage of a small family. They had to "penny-pinch" because they were paying a disproportionate amount of their income, over 40 percent, for housing. The average spent on housing at their income level in selected American cities ranged from 22 percent to 28 percent.[52] The Pennypackers exemplified a frequent characteristic of middle-class families. They were willing to sacrifice in many areas of their standard of living in order to own their home.

The real "nickel-stretchers" were the Kincaids of Oklahoma, who supported fifteen children on the same income on which the Pennypackers supported two, and the Millers of Harlem, who supported three children on 44 percent less. These families illustrated the two extremes of rural versus urban life. The Kincaids produced much of their own food and most of their own clothing. Staples produced outside of the home were purchased in large quantities. The Millers met their needs by renting out rooms. Besides their own family of five, another eight individuals lived in their five-room walk-up flat.[53]

Of these three families, the Pennypackers were most representative of the spending habits of American families. They had a particular value system which caused them to spend a disproportionate amount of their income on one aspect of family life—housing. Their values were personal and individualistic. No one could have convinced them that they spent too much on housing or that they might be more comfortable spending more on food, clothing, medical care, a savings account, or even recreation. Thus, families varied greatly in their attitudes toward different items of expenditure. Decisions on the distribution of family income were therefore a very personal family matter, whatever the prevailing value system may have been.

Problems emerged when family members differed in their values, especially if the various individuals had high standards in different areas. A popular novel of the thirties, *If I Had Four Apples*, by Josephine Lawrence, described the situation of a family called Hoe, in which the father was determined to own his home, although the rest of his family was not interested, and his payments actually cost him more than the house was worth. His values made it impossible for him to understand the seriousness of his economic situation: "You see, I don't believe in renting. A man with a family ought to own his own home. Not be paying his good money to landlords. Soon as things get a little better, I'll have my pay cuts back and I can swing it easy."[54]

Meanwhile, the mother was a very poor household manager who insisted upon good quality but was not above buying bad quality if it caught her fancy. To save money, she purchased things on sale in large quantities, whether she needed them or not. And she was self-righteous in her refusal to deny herself and her family: "I always say when we can't have what we want to eat life won't be worth living."[55] The three children of this unfortunate pair, who ranged from about fourteen years old to the early twenties, had all set unrealistically high goals for themselves in terms of jobs, careers, and material success. Everyone in the family was tied to different installment plans to satisfy his or her individual needs, and no one had the common sense to take over the financial management of the family.

The moral of the story reflected a fairly common understanding of the Depression. The Hoe family represented all of the worst habits of the new consumer society—bad management, unrealistic expectations, selfishness, and just plain stupidity. The not-too-subtle implication was that the personal suffering of the Depression had little to do with the working of the economic system. Rather, the greed and sheer incompetence of individuals was the source of bankruptcy and economic failure. In their ignorance of money matters, the Hoe family "lacked a savings or checking account. Rose and her husband, confusedly associating checks with the idea of credit, told each other they preferred to pay cash. They paid carrying charges with no idea of what the term signified, they practiced no fixed system of disbursement, nor had they any clear idea of their living expenses, much less their accumulated debt. The payment of small sums to as many creditors as possible, encouraged them to believe themselves solvent."[56]

Although the Hoe family was a caricature of American families, their attitudes and actions probably had some basis in reality. But the biggest obstacle facing most families who wished to balance the budget was a lack of money. A budget implies that there is room for flexibility with respect to expenditures, and although most families established priorities through the simple act of buying, few had a surplus requiring conscious decision or choice. As humorist Will Cuppy observed, "In order to run a budget you have to have money . . . I don't feel that I can afford one right now—there are so many other things I need worse." No doubt many Americans would have agreed with Cuppy, as well as sharing his attitude toward his own ineptitude: "I'm not good at figures, but I know when I'm ruined, and I don't have to write it down on a piece of paper."[57]

Although many families were living on a marginal basis during the Depression, they nevertheless managed to maintain a relatively high standard of living. The lower cost of living was one reason. Second, although the rate of consumption fell off considerably, especially during the early years of the Depression, the American people did not change their attitude toward material prosperity during these discouraging years. For many of them, installment buying remained an important means of maintaining a facsimile of the standard they wished to achieve (Appendix B).

Outwardly, many Americans were critical of the widespread use of credit during the 1920s and thirties, but this did not stop the majority of them from using it as a means of increasing their purchasing power. In January 1930, as the Depression intensified, the American people owed about $2.5 billion in installment debts, but according to a report in *Ladies' Home Journal*, this debt was paid with few defaults. Some 500 companies were financing installment buying at the time, and only five others had failed to survive the crash. Of every 100 accounts, only one resulted in a default. Although consumption of durable goods fell off steeply during the early thirties, by 1936 about $6 billion worth of automobiles, radios, and other goods were purchased by means of installment, a gain of 20 percent over 1929.[58]

A later study, done by the National Bureau of Economic Research, presented a more negative perspective on the use of credit during the Depression, although the two studies may have had different definitions of what constituted "credit" and "installment buying." According to the bureau's study, in spite of a striking increase in credit granted from 1932 to 1937, its volume in 1937 was approximately 15 percent below the 1929 peak. The recession in that year may have had an impact on the use of credit. Repayments during 1937 were 9 percent lower than in 1929, whereas average outstanding bills were 7 percent above 1929.[59]

A survey conducted by *Ladies' Home Journal* in 1938 revealed that more of their readers used installment buying than actually approved of it. Only 54 percent responding to a questionnaire approved of it, whereas 70 percent admitted to making installment purchases. An overwhelming majority of those using installment buying, or 88 percent, felt that it provided the family with things it would not have had otherwise.[60]

In other words, installment buying raised the material standard of living beyond the actual family income. It had the most far-reaching effects upon the lower income families. For the nonrelief population as a whole the gross addition to purchasing power resulting from the use of consumer credit in 1935-1936 came to less than 3 percent of the total income received, and after subtraction for repayments the net addition to income was less than 2 percent. However, the entire class of families with incomes under $500 added a net 10 percent to their immediate purchasing power through the use of consumer credit, and families with an income of $500 to $2,000 added from 2 percent to 5 percent. On the contrary, for

families receiving more than $2,000 a year, consumer credit was rela-
tively insignificant as a source of funds for additional spending (Appendix C).[61]

When families are considered in the aggregate with regard to income,
those who actually used consumer credit, or approximately one-third of
all nonrelief families, increased their spending capacity by more than 5
percent. Debtor families in the lowest income group, earning below $500,
annually supplemented their income by 38 percent; those in the $500 to
$750 group, by nearly 17 percent; and those with annual incomes of $750
to $1,000, by nearly 10 percent. The increase in momentary purchasing
power at the lower end of the income scale was significant for those who
were willing and able to take advantage of the opportunity. And in spite
of the setback to consumption provided by the Depression, the pressure
for a high standard of living remained. One Middletown woman
summed up the situation: "Most of the families I know are after the same
things today that they were after before the Depression, and they'll get
them in the same way—on credit."[62]

But credit also created problems, especially for the families of small
wage-earners, the very ones who benefited most from the system of
credit. The effects of financial overextension on the part of individual
families could be demoralizing. Emotional stress bordering upon a patho-
logical mental state, guilt, and friction between family members often led
to family breakdown. The problem was the result of ignorance or irresponsibility on the part of the customer, combined with the high pressure
tactics of salesmen which sometimes amounted to dishonesty. At least
one commentator felt that society in general had to share responsibility
for the client's weakness: "What can be said . . . of a civilization that con-
demns millions of willing and able workers to bare existence, through
inadequate wages, or even more inadequate relief without wages, and at
the same time parades before them the temptations of comforts and de-
cencies (to say nothing of luxuries) which are forbidden to them."[63]

Although financial overextension created problems for some families,
its only solution—a sharp reduction in consumption—involved problems
of its own and may well have been just as demoralizing. There was no
simple answer to the problem of income versus expenditure. It remained
up to the individual families, even if they were unable to budget, to determine some plan of financial management in order to escape complete
ruin. In most middle-class families the woman was the consumer manager. She did the shopping, managed the food and clothing, and was in
the best position to make savings in these areas.[64]

A 1939 study of 68 families who were successful in their families relations and money management revealed that most of them had a system of joint or mutual control of the family funds. In all but a few cases, the husband talked over his business affairs with the wife. The actual handling of money and the payment of bills seemed to be based on a division of labor. Men were more likely to make the payments on the house, interest, insurance, and coal. Women usually handled the payments on food, services, operating expenses except coal, and clothes and personal needs for herself and the children. In three-fifths of the families, joint decisions were made on all expenditures; in another one-sixth of the families this was true on all large items. On occasions when one spouse was dominant, it was because he or she was more interested or felt more responsible in a particular sphere.[65]

The man's sphere of financial management usually included items that were fixed expenditures. House payments and taxes involved no decisions, and although insurance might involve a decision with respect to amount, it was often a joint decision, made only a few times during the family cycle. Women, on the contrary, managed the expenditures that were flexible and could be manipulated to suit the current family needs.

A recognition of women's role in money management was implicit in nearly all of the articles written on the subject during th 1930s, and indeed all of the budget plans that appeared in popular journals were written by wives rather than husbands. Burr Blackburn, research director of the Household Finance Corporation, characterized the ideal family as one in which the man acted as "chairman of the board of directors and president," to be consulted on major policies, while the woman acted as "general manager and treasurer," to run the household, do the buying, and pay the bills. From Blackburn's point of view, financial jams were least likely to happen when the husband turned his paycheck over to the wife and delegated to her the authority to do the buying and pay the bills. Women were better buyers, closer spenders, and more conscientious about paying bills and making loan payments.[66]

Blackburn's positive analysis of women's fiscal abilities was not necessarily shared by his contemporaries, even those who acknowledged women's predominant role in spending. In Dayton, Ohio, a training school was established by local businessmen to teach women how to manage money.[67] But most of the advice to housewives was transmitted through popular reading materials, such as newspapers and magazines. And all of the personal accounts of family budgeting emphasized the woman's role in making over clothing, fixing cheap meals, and growing gardens. For better or worse, the man evidently played a small part in the budgeting procedure.

The emphasis upon household thrift and its beneficial effects on the standard of living was so strong that some observers felt that married women workers would be better off financially if they left their outside jobs to those who really needed them and expended all their energies on thriftiness within the home. This was one of the points made in the novel *If I Had Four Apples.*[68]

One of the most interesting attempts to dissuade married women from working was launched by Mrs. Ralph Borsodi, whose husband, a leader of the "homestead" movement during the Depression, had written several books spelling out the disaster and ugliness of the technological age and urging a return to small farming and domestic production as a security against the fluctuations of the business cycle. Borsodi, in keeping with her husband's belief in domestic production, conducted a personal experiment to prove that working women could actually earn more by doing productive work at home. She fed her family of four a diet recommended by the United States Department of Agriculture for $10.90 per week. The diet was estimated to cost $16.50 a week based on average retail prices in the United States for May 7, 1935. Thus, the woman who invested her time in baking and cooking could save $5.60 per week, or about half the earnings of the average woman worker working 44 to 48 hours a week. And the amount could be earned in less than three hours a day.[69]

But Borsodi's experience was not applicable to all married women workers. In particular, it was not relevant to women making the average wage of $10 to $12 a week, since they were probably at the low or lower-middle income levels. According to the study of consumer purchases, the average expenditure on food did not reach $10 a week until the family income level of $1,250 to $1,499. And the average family spending $16.00 a week on groceries was also earning about $2,500.[70] Thus, the great majority of American women were not in a position to spend Borsodi's upper figure, and less than half of them were spending what she considered to be the thrift budget.

Moreover, Borsodi attributed her success in homemaking to the use of modern kitchen appliances which greatly increased her efficiency. These included an electric range, electric refrigeration, and an electric mixer. Admittedly the kitchen represented a large investment, but Borsodi saw it as an investment that paid for itself, not a luxury. Kitchen appliances, she maintained, "not only 'earn their keep'; they are my answer to the charge that doing housework must inflict a painful amount of drudgery on women."

Borsodi's objectives were more than economic. She insisted that the revival of home production would have great social significance, particularly if accompanied by a recognition of the economic importance of women's role. Home production "would do more to re-establish women's rights than any amount of tinkering with political office or struggling for equal pay." A return to household industry would restore" the social balance which women's acceptance of industrial civilization has shattered."[71]

Yet few American women were able to afford Borsodi's kitchen conveniences without working for them outside of the home, and few could be expected to have either her aptitude or her enthusiasm for household production. True, most of the women who wrote personal accounts of their budgeting efforts were engaged in home production, but these were not women who had given up jobs. They were in the middle and upper income levels so that they had a fairly flexible income with which they could buy both conveniences and commodities.

Borsodi, like so many of her contemporaries, misrepresented the reasons women worked. She was speaking to a minority when she argued that women who were leaving the home to escape male domination were merely shifting that dominance from the home to the office. Women had many unspoken personal reasons for engaging in work outside the home, but during the 1930s the overwhelming reason was still economic. Economic need may have included many of the appliances that Borsodi took for granted, and it may have included the freedom to purchase prepared food at the grocery store rather than spending several hours a day preparing it; but it nonetheless was primarily economics that impelled women to work.

Those who argued that women would be better off economically if they stayed in the home misinterpreted not only the economic nature of the female work force but also the psychology of family life in the 1920s and 1930s. The American people had grown accustomed either to owning or to wanting many of the luxuries and conveniences of the industrial age. But most Americans could not afford them on the wages of one family member. Particularly during the Depression, it became necessary to depend upon other family members to support even a declining standard of living. Budgeting was a possibility for those with enough money to budget, but for others, an additional income, no matter how small, seemed the most practical solution.

3

Mothers and Children

Economic and social change are often closely intertwined, and this is particularly true with respect to family values. [American families of the 1920s and 1930s who aspired to a particular standard of living defined that standard not only in terms of material effects but also in terms of what they considered to be desirable family roles.] Ideally, most families of the broad middle-class and those aspiring to it wished their children to remain children, either at home or in school, and wished their wives and mothers to remain within the home caring for the family, but most particularly for the children. [The child-rearing role, and thus the mother-child relationship, became the focus of the family.] The emphasis on this relationship reflected a shift in the nature of the household economy. This was a long-range historical development that occurred over a period of more than a century, and it had a direct impact upon individual families according to their class, race, ethnicity, and geographical region.[1]

However, it was not always possible to meet the ideal of the mother-child relationship, even for those families who professed loyalty to it. As the household economy lost its productive role and increased its consumption of purchased goods, additional income beyond that of the principal wage-earner became more important rather than less. There was a basic dilemma in this need for additional wage-earners at a time when the role of women and children in the home was glorified, and when women's domestic role, with respect both to housekeeping and to child care, was greatly intensified. [Economic needs and social values came into direct conflict for the family that aspired to middle-class standards in both spheres.]

Two demographic trends of the early twentieth century reflected the changed attitude toward children's role in the family. One was the rapid decline in the birth rate between 1910 and 1940, and the other was the decline in child labor, which was particularly sharp during the 1920s and

1930s. The first of these trends had a direct impact on women's domestic role; the second may well have affected women's economic role outside of the home.

The decline in the birth rate was part of a long-term trend that had begun in the early nineteenth century; in fact, the bulk of the decline as measured by ratios of young children to white women occurred before 1900, with a considerable amount occurring before the mid-century. But the decline became more rapid in the two decades preceding 1940. In 1910 the birth rate was 30.1 per thousand population, and by 1940 it was down to 19.4. The decline resulted in a decrease in the numbers of children per adult women as well as a decline in the actual number of births. Until the 1920s the estimated number of births had increased with each census, in spite of the declining birth rate, but during the twenties, for the first time in American history the number of white births declined.[2]

The American tendency toward smaller families during the early decades of the twentieth century reflected a recognition that children were no longer an asset to the household economy. It also indicated that Americans who aspired to a middle-class standard of living felt that children needed the emotional and material benefits that were difficult, if not impossible, to bestow upon them in a large family with many children.[3]

Although many long-range casual factors contributed to the declining birth rate over time, the controversial issue of the 1920s was birth control. The morality of birth control was a topic of debate, but clinics were nonetheless opened in various large cities during the decade. They served a basically working-class clientele, since the middle class was more apt to visit private doctors rather than clinics. The birth control movement made its greatest strides during the Depression, both in terms of professionalization and in numbers of clinics. In 1930 there were only 40 medically directed birth control clinics in the United States. By 1937 there were 288 in 40 states and the District of Columbia. One clinic, in Sioux Falls, Iowa, was even established in the city hall.[4] There is no way of knowing just how many people were practicing birth control. The several studies made suggest that very few people of any class were using contraceptives on a steady and regular basis during the 1920s.[5] Thus birth control, as a technique, can be considered as only one of many factors contributing to a long-term decline in the birth rate.

Women may have had fewer children to care for in the 1920s and 1930s, but this did not mean that they spent less time caring for them. A new concentration on children, stimulated by environmental social theories and the rise of social psychology, had a strong impact on attitudes toward the parents' role in child nurture. Children were recognized as developing individuals who required treatment different from that accorded adults. This was the essential principle behind all child welfare programs. The new profession of social casework increased the burdens of parenthood by emphasizing the influence of early childhood on later life.[6]

The development of social psychology influenced the rise of behaviorism, a derivation of animal psychology which explained the behavior of humans in terms of stimulus and response rather than ideas. John B. Watson, founder of the behaviorist school in America, argued that all human functions, including thinking, could be observed and controlled scientifically. It thus was possible to control the training of a child so as to determine exactly the adult he or she would become. Watson's *Psychological Care of Infant and Child*, which appeared in 1928, was extremely influential in persuading conscientious mothers of the seriousness of their maternal duties. He insisted upon a fixed schedule of feeding and sleeping for the infant and opposed the coddling of children. Mothers anxiously watched their clocks, avoided spoiling their children, and in general did their best to abide by Watsonian principles of child care.[7]

The growing interest in child care was reflected in the progress made in parent education during the 1920s. By 1930 parent education programs were in operation in twenty-two states. Six universities and two schools for social work offered graduate professional training for parent education workers. There was a growing number of lectures, discussion groups, university correspondence courses, syndicated newspaper columns, and magazine articles directed at parents. The subject matter indicated a trend away from physical care and habit training toward personality and character formation as well as social adjustment.[8]

Parental concern for children was mirrored by increased community involvement through the child welfare movement, health centers, playgrounds, youth organizations, camps, and religious agencies. Thus, the home and family were supplemented by other agencies for certain aspects of child care. But while the mother of the 1920s may have seen less of her children because of their involvement in school and community, and while she may have had access to many resources for information and assistance, she was also under a great deal of pressure to produce happy and well-adjusted children under conditions that were complicated and, in some ways, almost revolutionary. A Middletown mother expressed her confusion: "Life was simpler for my mother . . . In those days one did not realize that there was so much to be known about the care of children. I realize that I ought to be half a dozen experts, but I'm afraid of making mistakes and usually do not know where to go for advice."[9]

The real problem of child care in the 1920s and 1930s, at least for the middle-class mother, was one of high expectations and bewilderment as to the best way to achieve them. [A similar intensification of expectations influenced women in their attitudes toward housework.] The significant difference in housekeeping during this period was not so much in the time involved as in the range of tasks. A typical housewife of the 1920s might do a wider variety of activities in a single day than her nineteenth-century predecessor, but she probably spent less time on each. Also, she had more choices as to how she wanted to spend her time. Not everyone sewed; not everyone baked. Some had many children and gave them little time; others had few children and gave them much time. A study done in 1929 reported a range in number of hours spent per week on housework from a minimum of 44.3 hours to a maximum of 87.5 hours for woman who did a great deal of gardening and canning.[10]

Both rural and urban homemakers spent, on the average, similar amounts of time on homemaking chores, but the amount of time spent on specific tasks varied greatly from rural to urban areas. The family sociologist William Ogburn found that in the city homes, housewives spent 56 hours and 39 minutes a week on homemaking duties, while farm wives spent 53 hours and 50 minutes. The surprising fact is that the time spent by city wives exceeded that spent by farm wives. The explanation lies in the comparison of time spent on specific duties. For instance, the percentage of time spent on preparing meals and washing dishes was less in the city homes than on the farms—33 percent as compared with 43 percent. The allotment for housecleaning was about the same for both—13 percent and 14 percent, respectively. Washing and ironing required a smaller proportion of time in the city than on the farm—8 percent and 10 percent. Only 23 percent of the city homes did all of their washing at home, as compared with 70 percent of the farm homes. Mending and sewing also occupied a smaller proportion of the time of the city household than of the farm household—6 percent and 9 percent.

These tasks comprised a large part of the production of essential economic goods and services. The women in city homes spent 63 percent of their total homemaking time on these basic chores, whereas farm families spent 82 percent. The remaining time was spent on the care of children, purchasing and management, going back and forth, and other homemaking activities. To these duties, city homemakers gave proportionally much more attention than did their rural counterparts.[11]

[Technological developments which affected change in the function of the housewife tended to have their greatest impact upon expectations of what it meant to be a good homemaker rather than upon time spent on that particular occupation.] Although the urban housewife with her numerous conveniences had less of the drudgery of housework, this change was in degree only, and it was compensated for by an increased level of activity in other areas. Different things were expected of the housewife in terms of management, consumption, child care, and community activity as a consequence of social and technological change.

Perhaps the key word was "flexibility," the ability to determine priorities according to family and individual needs. But homemaking remained a full-time occupation, and the woman who tried to combine an outside job or career with her homemaking duties most probably exhausted herself while still failing to live up to the standards of her contemporaries.

In view of the difficulties of combining home and job, it is a wonder that married women entered the labor force at all during the 1920s and 1930s. The combination of economic need and new employment opportunities provided the essential elements in drawing women out of their homes, even as they felt the continuing need to fulfill their roles as housewives and mothers. Economic need, which is always relative, was during the 1920s in particular a reflection of new standards of living. But an individual family's definition of need may have been related to the fact that most successful middle-income families had several wage-earners, and as child labor became less common among aspiring middle-class families, the wife and mother sometimes had to fill an economic role once performed by older sons and daughters.

Most married women workers were supplementary wage-earners, but without that supplementary wage, an individual family might have been low-income rather than middle-income, since it is possible that the husband's earnings were inadequate in themselves to support family standards. There is evidence to suggest a direct relationship between higher income level and the number of earners in nonfarm families at the various wage or salary income levels (Table 3.1).

To a surprising extent, middle-income families derived their status through the efforts of several family members. At the very low wage and salary levels, less than one out of five families had an extra wage-earner, but nearly one out of four families earning $800 to $1,600 relied on an extra wage-earner. A substantial increase in the proportion of families with extra earners occurred after $1,600. And these categories did not represent an insignificant number of families, for 22 percent of all urban

Table 3.1. Urban and rural nonfarm families by earners and family income, 1939

Income level ($)	Distribution (%)	Families with 2 or more earners (%)
0	5.6	—
Under 199	2.9	7.2
200-399	6.0	13.8
400-599	7.2	17.8
600-799	8.1	19.4
800-999	7.4	23.3
1,000-1,199	7.8	24.4
1,200-1,399	8.7	23.9
1,400-1,599	8.1	26.8
1,600-1,999	11.9	35.3
2,000-2,499	10.7	41.5
2,500-2,999	5.5	55.3
3,000-4,999	7.3	60.7
5,000 and over	1.7	46.5
Not reported	1.1	—
Total	100.0	28.6

Source: Sixteenth Census of the United States, 1940. Population, Families: Family Wage or Salary Income in 1939 (Washington, D.C.: Government Printing Office, 1943), pp. 32-33.

and rural nonfarm families had wage or salary incomes between $1,600 and $2,500 in 1939, and over one-third of them relied upon several family earners. [Thus many American families owed their middle-class consumption patterns not to adequate wages for one person but to the presence of several wage-earners in the family.]

In spite of traditional American values that support the ideal of the one-wage-earner family, most families have always depended upon the economic contributions of several members. Sometimes this contribution took the form of "unpaid family work," as in the case of the agricultural family or the family that ran its own business. But families in the wage-earning class were also many times dependent upon the efforts of all those able to work. In 1930, 31.9 percent of all American families had two or more wage-earners. By the 1940 census the figure was down to 25.1 percent, which was a considerable decline but nonetheless left one family out of every four living on the income of several wage-earners.[12]

Although the decline in the proportion of families with extra wage-earners could have been related to the general unemployment that was still a problem in 1940, it more likely reflected the rapid decline in the number of gainfully occupied children during the first half of the twentieth century (Table 3.2). The census report of 1920 attributed the sudden decline in child labor between 1910 and 1920 to the change in the date of the census from a busy farming season in 1910 (April 15) to a very slow farming season in 1920 (January 1), as well as to the increased legal restrictions against child labor, better-enforced compulsory school attendance laws, and more efficient enforcement of both classes of laws.[13] The legal factors were probably more important than the seasonal influence, since they were part of the long-term trend. By 1940 children below the age of fourteen were not even considered in labor force statistics, and children between the ages of fourteen and seventeen had further decreased their labor force participation (Table 3.3). Although the younger age group, ten to fifteen years old, had shown its most dramatic decline before 1920, the groups above fourteen years continued a fairly high rate of decline through the 1920s and 1930s. In 1920, 31 percent of the fourteen- to nineteen-year-old age group were gainfully employed, but the figure dropped to 20.4 percent in 1930 and 13.2 percent in 1940.

Child labor, as a social problem, had hardly been solved by the 1920s and 1930s; in fact, during the 1930s abuses of child labor laws were especially prevalent. But by this time the problem had become primarily racial and regional, rooted in the economic and social conditions of the American South. In 1930 only 1.5 percent of white children ages ten to thirteen were at work. The proportion of black children workers of the

Table 3.2. Percentage of children 10-15 years old of both sexes in the labor force, 1880-1930

Year	% total population	% male population	% female population
1880	16.8	24.4	9.0
1890	18.1	25.9	10.0
1900	18.2	26.1	10.2
1910	18.4	24.8	11.9
1920	8.5	11.3	5.6
1930	4.7	6.4	2.9

Source: 1930 Census, Population, vol. V, *General Report on Occupations* (Washington, D.C.: Government Printing Office, 1933), p. 45.

Table 3.3. Percentage of children 14-19 years old of both sexes in the labor force, 1900-1940

Age	1900	1910	1920	1930	1940
14-15	30.9	30.7	17.5	9.2	5.2
Male	43.4	41.4	23.3	12.6	8.0
Female	18.2	19.8	11.6	5.8	2.2
16-17	—	—	44.7	31.7	21.0
Male	—	—	38.0	41.2	29.0
Female	—	—	31.6	22.1	12.9
18-19	—	—	60.0	55.3	52.7
Male	—	—	78.3	70.7	65.6
Female	—	—	42.3	40.5	40.5

Source: 1940 Census, Population, vol. III, *The Labor Force,* pt. I, *U.S. Summary,* p. 26. The census data, however, did not disclose all the ways in which children earned money, such as working during summer vacation. Investigations by federal agencies and social agencies revealed that many thousands of children were working in sugar beet fields, cranberry bogs, cotton plantations, and other forms of industrialized agriculture, as well as in street trades, tenement home work, domestic service, and canneries. See Hazel Kyrk, *Economic Problems of the Family* (New York: Harper & Bros., 1929), pp. 133-134; Walter I. Trattner, *Crusade for the Children: A History of the National Child Labor Reform in America* (Chicago: Quadrangle Books, 1970), ch. 6.

same age group was 11 percent. White children ages fourteen and fifteen had 5 percent in the work force; for black children the proportion was 23 percent. Agriculture was the primary employer of black children, occupying 85 percent of those who were in the work force. And 98 percent of gainfully occupied black children were in the southern census districts.[14]

The occupational and racial characteristics of the child labor force were reflected in the census data of 1940, which showed the relationship to the head of the household of all those participating in the labor force. Young people, particularly young men, were still more apt to be gainfully employed during the 1920s and 1930s than were homemakers. Most of the extra family wage-earners were not wives or mothers but other relatives of the head of the household, usually children (Table 3.4).[15]

The data, which proves that most extra family wage-earners were not wives and mothers, might also suggest that male teenagers under the age of eighteen were more likely to bring in extra income than were their

Table 3.4.   Persons other than head of household in the labor force by age and sex, 1940

Relationship to head	No. in labor force (millions)	% in labor force
Wife	3.29	12.5
Other relative		
Male, 14-17 years	.87	18.4
Male, 18 and over	8.99	79.0
Female, 14-17 years	.37	7.2
Female, 18 and over	4.50	56.7

Source: Sixteenth Census of the United States, 1940. Population: The Labor Force (Sample Statistics), Employment and Personal Characteristics (Washington, D.C.: Government Printing Office, 1943), p. 55.

mothers, but the nature of the boys' employment suggests otherwise. Young boys were much more likely to be listed as "unpaid family workers," and though their economic contribution may have been considerable in this capacity, it is doubtful that it exceeded the economic role of the homemaker in all the occupational groupings (Table 3.5). The significant occupational fields for the wives of heads of household were clerical and sales work, factory operation, and service work, with over half of the last group found in service other than domestic. Young girls listed as "other relatives" were most likely to be domestic servants or farm laborers, although a significant proportion were factory operatives or clerical and sales workers. Young boys had the most concentrated occupational distribution, with nearly 60 percent classified as farm laborers. They were also engaged as laborers, other than farm, factory operatives, and clerical and sales workers, but their heavy concentration in farm work bears out the high percentage that were classified as "unpaid family workers." If that category were left out, and if only wage or salary workers and employers or self-employed were considered, only 6.1 percent of all boys between the ages of fourteen and seventeen would be included. On the contrary, 10.8 percent of all wives of household heads would be included.[16] Thus, by 1940, married homemakers were more likely to be making an economic contribution through paid employment than were their children, either male or female, under the age of eighteen.

Although the actual employment of family members suggests an eco-

Table 3.5.   Persons other than head of household in the labor force, by class and occupation, 1940

		Other relative of head	
Occupation	Wife of head	Female (14-17)	Male (14-17)
Class			
Wage and salary workers	81.0	76.4	50.2
Employers and self-employed	11.0	0.9	2.7
Unpaid family workers	8.0	22.7	47.0
Total	100.0	100.0	100.0
Occupation			
Professionals, semiprofessionals	9.1	0.8	0.2
Farmers, farm managers	0.6	0.1	1.0
Proprietors, managers, officials	5.8	0.1	0.3
Clerical and sales workers	25.6	13.4	12.2
Craftsmen, foremen	1.3	0.2	1.2
Factory operatives	25.9	14.5	10.5
Domestic workers	11.9	29.6	0.1
Service workers except domestic	12.4	7.5	4.5
Farm laborers and foremen	4.0	26.5	59.5
Other laborers and unknown	3.6	7.3	9.9
Total	100.0	100.0	100.0

Source: Sixteenth Census of the United States, 1940. Population: The Labor Force, p. 137.

nomic contribution, it is not a completely reliable measure of responsibility for family support as shared by its members. Although employed homemakers were likely to be supplementary rather than principal wage-earners, most young people had even less responsibility for household finances. Much depended on the family income level, its occupational status, and personal family feelings, particularly with respect to values and goals. In some cases, an employed young person might be expected only to provide his own clothing and spending money, which in itself represented a savings for the family. But in other cases, he might be expected to turn over all of his earnings to his parents, or to pay his room and board, contribute to a specific family goal such as buying a house or a business, or help a sibling with education. Young people enjoyed a wider variety of possible uses for their money than did married women, who usually contributed all of their earnings to family support.[17]

The economic contribution of women and young people reflected, in addition to individual family values, a wide range of ethnic traditions. The relationship between work, race, and ethnicity is an extremely complicated paradigm which has been the topic of several studies. Virginia Yans-McLauglin, who has done extensive work on the Italian family, observed that Italian children working in canneries were expected to work and travel with their parents, and that Italians mothers pushed their children harder and expected more work of them than did American parents. Tamara Hareven argued that in the textile community of Manchester, New Hampshire, the French Canadian immigrants had the highest average number of family members working in the textile industry, or 3.9 members in a family. Children were socialized to the work experience in the mill at an early age through the work of their parents, and the family economy, as well as its work ethnic, was built on the assumption that children would contribute to the family's income from the earliest possible age. Claudia Goldin, in a study of the labor force participation of children in Philadelphia in 1880, concluded that Irish and German children were in the labor force to a greater degree than native white children, and that they contributed a larger percentage of the family income.[18]

The efforts of the Children's Bureau to document children's work in the twentieth century also support the conclusion that the children of immigrants were more likely to be in the work force than those of native parentage. A study of Boston working children published in 1922 indicated that although only about one-fifth of the working children who were surveyed were foreign-born, nearly three-fourths, or 72.1 percent, had foreign-born fathers. In an anthracite coal field district of Pennsylvania, 50.4 percent of the children with foreign-born fathers were doing regular work, as compared with 30.2 percent of the children with native-born fathers. Also, the percentage of these children who went to work before their fourteenth birthday was larger among the children of foreign-born fathers, or 25.9 percent, as compared to 10.5 percent for children of native-born fathers.[19]

Unfortunately, the issue of ethnicity received little attention in the census reports of 1930 and 1940, as least as far as it affected employment of young people. In 1930, foreign-born white children ten to seventeen years of age had a higher proportion in the labor force than native whites, or 17.1 percent, as compared to 9.7 percent for native whites and 23.6 percent for blacks. But there was no breakdown by parentage, so that there is no way of knowing the impact of ethnicity upon American-born youngsters.[20]

Ethnicity had little effect on the over-all work experience of married women. Although there was considerable variation among nationalities, foreign-born women in general had a labor force participation rate very similar to that of native women. In 1920, native white married women were in the labor force at the rate of 6.3 percent, regardless of whether their parents were foreign-born or native-born. Of foreign-born married women, 7.2 percent were engaged in gainful occupations. These figures do not take into account the many ways in which married women supplemented family income through home industries, boarding and lodging operations, or occasional work outside of the home. But whatever their economic activity, married women were much more likely to contribute all of their earnings directly to the family than were employed young people.[21]

Thus, the employed homemaker was much more important to the economic well-being of her family than were her working children. She played a double economic role—one at home and one on the job. She was more likely to be working outside of the home for wages, and she contributed all of her earnings to family needs.

Many times family needs were actually children's needs, not only in the material sense but also in the educational sense. By the late nineteenth and early twentieth centuries, schooling or some kind of vocational training was becoming more and more important to middle-class youth as a means of avoiding dead-end careers. Even among the working class education took on a new significance, and many mothers worked to keep their children in parochial schools.[22]

[Although no direct relationship can be shown to exist between the decline of child labor and the rise in the number of married working women, it is possible that wives and mothers moved into the labor force in unconscious response to the withdrawal of children.[Certainly both of these developments—the decline of child labor and the movement of married women into the labor force—reflected changing attitudes toward family roles through a process of modernization.] The irony is that women of the aspiring middle class and the lower-middle class were caught in a double bind as they were forced to choose between the dictates of home and the marketplace. Although during the 1920s and 1930s these women were still in a distinct minority, they were the advance wave of the post-World War II flood of working women.

4

The Married Woman Worker

[The long-term trend in the employment of married women, together with its impact upon the roles of women and children, was a part of the process of economic modernization (Table 4.1). The married woman worker of the 1920s and 1930s was propelled into gainful employment by a variety of factors, but the most important factor was the changing nature of the household economy in terms of a decrease of production and an increase in consumption.]Few Americans were able to understand the implications of these changes for women's economic role. Instead, those hostile to married women workers accused them of undermining the stability of the home and taking jobs from men and unmarried women; whereas those sympathetic to married women workers argued that wives and mothers worked only out of necessity, and they condemned an economic system that forced women into these unwanted roles. [Many argued that as most women had someone to support them, they were therefore working only for "pin money." The "pin-money theory" was also the justification for lower wages.] Even during the 1920s and back into the nineteenth century, this argument was advanced by antifeminists and others who felt threatened by women's changing roles, and it was accepted by almost everyone except social reformers and labor reformers. Mary Anderson, director of the Women's Bureau, felt that the "pin-money theory" was one of the most exasperating problems facing those who tried to advance the cause of working women.[1]

The Women's Bureau, as a strong advocate of women's right to work, was particularly concerned with disproving the "pin-money theory." During the 1920s and 1930s the bureau conducted a number of surveys and studies of particular cities and industries for the express purpose of proving that working women, both married and single, were working out of economic necessity.[2] By the 1930s the debate had both intensified and expanded. A letter from a man in Houston, Texas, that appeared in a

Table 4.1. Women in the labor force by marital condition, 1890-1940

Marital condition	Total (millions)	Gainfully occupied		
		Millions	%	% distribution
1890				
Females over 14	19.6	3.7	18.9	100.0
Single and unknown	6.3	2.5	40.5	68.2
Married	11.1	0.5	4.6	13.9
Widowed and divorced	2.2	0.7	29.9	17.9
1900				
Females over 14	24.2	4.9	20.6	100.0
Single and unknown	7.6	3.3	43.5	66.2
Married	13.8	0.77	5.6	15.4
Widowed and divorced	2.8	0.9	32.5	18.4
1910				
Females over 14	3.1	7.6	25.4	100.0
Single and unknown	9.0	4.6	51.1	60.2
Married	17.7	1.9	10.7	24.7
Widowed and divorced	3.4	1.2	34.1	15.0
1920				
Females over 14	35.2	8.3	23.7	100.0
Single, widowed, divorced, and unknown	13.9	6.4	46.4	77.0
Married	21.4	1.9	9.0	23.0
1930				
Females over 14	42.8	10.6	24.8	100.0
Single and unknown	11.4	5.7	50.5	53.9
Married	26.2	3.1	11.7	28.9
Widowed and divorced	5.3	1.8	34.4	17.2
1940				
Females over 13	50.5	12.8	25.3	100.0
Single	13.9	6.4	45.0	49.4
Married	30.1	4.6	15.3	35.5
Husband present	28.5	3.8	13.3	29.6
Husband absent	1.6	.75	46.9	5.9
Widowed and divorced	6.5	1.9	29.2	15.1

Source: Sixteenth Census of the United States, 1940. Population, vol. III, *The Labor Force,* pt. I, *U.S. Summary,* p. 26; *Fifteenth Census of the United States, 1930,* vol. V, *General Report on Occupations,* p. 272; Gertrude Bancroft, *The American Labor Force: Its Growth and Changing Composition,* Census Monograph Series (New York: John Wiley & Sons, 1958), p. 45.

1933 *Literary Digest* prompted a varied response from readers which touched on the main points of both sides of the argument. The letter proclaimed that "Married women workers with other means of support can render a patriotic service to our President and the NRA during this economic crisis by withdrawing from the field of gainful employment." This would result, the letter continued, in "several millions of people being self-sustaining, who are now dependent upon charity, and those giving up the jobs would not be deprived of any of the necessities of life."[3]

Over the next two months eleven letters to the editor appeared debating the issue, five of them supporting the letter writer's position, five of them supporting women's right to work, and one from a man suggesting that all work be turned over to women on the grounds that men had supported women for centuries, and it was "high time" they had a rest. "If some women like to work so well, let them go to it."[4] Letters opposed to married women workers called them "leeches" and "moral parasites"— women without honor who often had better homes and better cars than their employers. Those who supported women's right to work argued that the problem was not that of too many women working but that of too many people not working.

The views that were aired in this interchange reflected the arguments of the more sophisticated commentators who wrote for the popular and learned journals. The writers who supported women's right to work took the position that married women workers were not the cause of unemployment, that most married women worked out of economic necessity and that their work actually created jobs for others by stimulating demand. If extreme need was to be the sole basis of married women's employment, then the same standard of need should hold for men's and single women's employment.[5]

[Those critical of married women workers took a somewhat more complicated position that went beyond the economics of unemployment to the more emotional issue of home, family, and motherhood.] The perspective of these critics differed in that they were attacking a particular class of married women workers, the "career women" who worked for fulfillment and for the luxuries of life rather than for a living.[6] Their opponents, the reformers who supported women's right to work, concentrated on the women in the lower economic stratum. [The whole issue, as presented by both sides, involved moral attitudes and values regarding the role of women in the family and in the broader society.]

For instance, a contributor to the labor journal *American Federationist* linked the salvation of civilization, as well as mere economic recovery, to the protection of children, their mothers, and their homes: "Woman's greatest security is to be found in the home, and where rests the security of women rests the security of life, the security of civilization." This eloquent spokesman for women's well-being advocated a "wage-equalization tariff" equivalent to 90 percent of the wages of the married woman worker. He noted optimistically that "this tax is so high that it will drive all married women out of industry."[7]

The proposed solution underscored both the sentiment attached to women's family role and the fear that women were undercutting men in the labor market. Reformers and social workers often expressed a similar sentiment with respect to women's family role, but they felt that married women workers were forced out of their homes and into the workplace by poverty, not by choice. Throughout the early decades of the twentieth century, considerable evidence was collected to support this theory. In 1914 Katharine Anthony, under the aegis of the Russell Sage Foundation, conducted a door-to-door survey of the Middle West Side district of New York City. She found that less than half of the married working women had husbands who contributed to family support, and nearly one-third were widows. In families where the husband was at work, he earned less than $500 a year, and the earnings of the mother, and sometimes of children, were essential to the support of the family.[8]

During the 1920s and 1930s the Women's Bureau actively pursued evidence of economic need among working women. From 1919 to 1929 the bureau conducted twenty-five studies that were directly concerned with the marital status and the living and working conditions of gainfully occupied women. The studies were unrepresentative of the female work force as a whole, since they tended to focus upon light industries, such as candy making, fruit growing and canning, textile manufacturing, cotton milling, and laundering. These were the industries that employed large numbers of women, but they were also likely to employ women of low economic status. Married women and women who were widowed and divorced were overrepresented in comparison to their numbers in the work force as a whole. In the 25 studies done between 1919 and 1929, 46.7 percent of over 165,000 women were either married or had been married, and 17.5 percent were widowed or divorced. In ten of the studies, women who had never married were less than 50 percent of the group, and in three studies the proportion dropped below 35 percent.[9]

The attempt to determine why women worked was carried on by a variety of groups and individuals. The question was in fact considered a major social issue during these years. But those concerned with women's right to work failed to differentiate between relative and absolute need. They tended to emphasize the role that absolute need played in pushing women into the labor force, while ignoring the possibility of their wish to achieve a higher standard of living. A consideration of the married woman worker and economic need requires a differentiation between absolute need at the poverty level and relative need at every other level. Although the poverty-stricken contributed more than their share to the married-women work force during these years, the higher standards of living that working-class and middle-class families tried to maintain forced many married women into gainful employment when their need was relative rather than absolute.

For instance, a 1930 study made by the industrial department of the YWCA uncovered ten reasons mentioned by 519 married women for their gainful employment. The women in this group were primarily factory workers, but there were also household employees, telephone operators, and a few low-paid clerical workers. They were selected from 19 states and 66 widely scattered communities. Over 70 percent of the workers were living with their husbands, and 68 percent had children. About 44 percent of the women in this sample, or 232 people, worked because they felt that their family income was "insufficient." About 38 percent worked because their husband was ill, unemployed, or no longer living with the family. This group displayed conclusive economic need, since the woman was probably the only wage-earner in the family. But in the case of those who felt that their family income was insufficient, the degree of economic need is not easily determined. It must have varied considerably among the 232 respondents. Other reasons given, such as "Had to pay debts," would be subject to the same uncertainty.

The substantial number of women who admitted that they were working for reasons other than absolute necessity is more revealing than the even higher number who claimed necessity. Three less essential economic needs—namely saving money, educating children, and buying "extras"— were cited by 548 respondents. Although these are admirable and justifiable reasons for working, they indicate rising expectations with regard to a standard of living and future provisions over and above pure economic necessity.[10]

In spite of the fact that these women were involved in low status jobs with low pay—the median pay was $16 a week, but nearly half made $15 or less—over one-fourth of the workers mentioned interest in their job as one of their reasons for working. At a time when most married women were concentrated in the less desirable occupational fields, a large number of them derived satisfaction from the job itself, or from the social intercourse that it offered, beyond a mere paycheck. The extent to which women actually enjoyed their work was a factor greatly neglected by Women's Bureau investigators and others concerned with disproving the "pin money theory." They generally assumed that a married women, particularly one with children, would stay home if she had a husband able and willing to support her.[11] This may have been more true for the women in industry than for those in white-collar and professional occupations, but in any case it was not generally true.

Frances Donovan, a Chicago high school teacher who spent two summers working with saleswomen, wrote a rosy account of the independence of the salesgirl, her satisfaction with her job, and her ability successfully to combine career and marriage. Donovan cited a number of related reasons for the married woman's return to a job, including the loneliness at home, the atmosphere on the job, the wages that could be used to buy luxuries, and the desire for recognition: "The store and their encounter with the real world had made them free souls and women of the world." The department store offered a particularly convenient job for the married woman because much of the work was part-time. Donovan argued that the part-time job facilitated rather than hindered marriage and that half of the women employed in stores were married.[12]

Lorine Pruette, the author of several books on working women, saw the part-time job as a way of strengthening the home by allowing women, as well as men, to find their major occupational interest in the world outside. Thus, the modern home would become a place of refuge for both men and women in which it did not matter who did the cooking or the laundry. Although Pruette greatly exaggerated the degree to which the burdens of housework had become a thing of the past, she made two points contrary to the basic assumptions of most social workers and the investigators at the Women's Bureau. First, she suggested that many women were working to fulfill a demand for luxuries: "The two-car family, by and large, demands the two-wage family." Second, she argued that many women found work fulfilling in itself. This was the position taken by many of the career feminists during these years, and there is evidence to suggest that for business and professional women this was probably true.[13]

A study of marriage and careers done by Virginia MacMakin Collier in 1926 indicated that professional women were more likely to be motivated to work by the need for activity or contacts than by financial necessity. But only 100 women were included in the study, and 72 percent of them earned more than $2,000 a year.[14] The group was so select that it could hardly throw much light upon the motivating factors of the great mass of working women. Although the Collier group was not typical of American working women, it was considered typical by many people of both the feminist and conservative persuasions. Sympathizers of women workers sought to destroy this view of the woman worker as belonging to the privileged class in order to undermine the pin-money theory. In their attempt to do so, they sometimes accepted at face value the economic need of the women they studied.

A study by Cecile T. LaFollette in 1932 reflects this tendency. The group surveyed included 652 women of the business and professional class, and 438 of them, or 67 percent, gave "economic necessity" as their reason for working. Many of the other reasons given were really economic in character, such as to educate the children, make payments on the house, pay for sickness or college debts, and raise the standard of living. For instance, 320 women, or 49 percent, worked in order to provide the "extras" that would not have been possible on their husband's salary alone.[15]

Many of the women who gave "economic necessity" as their reason for working must have stretched the term to include some of these other items. Although LaFollette felt that the incomes of the husbands offered ample evidence that most of these women had to work, the distribution by their husband's incomes suggests otherwise (Table 4.2). Most of these families were far better off than their contemporaries. As the LaFollette study was done in 1932, which was the low point of the Depression, the income levels are somewhat comparable to those of 1935-1936.

LaFollette declared that no one would question "why the wives of the 41 husbands who make less than $1,000 or the 166 who make from $1,000 to $2,000 are gainfully employed," because these families would be below a bare subsistence level if the wives were not gainfully employed. But 42 percent of all American families at the time in fact had incomes under $1,000, and 80 percent were under $2,000. Even among nonrelief families, 35 percent had incomes under $1,000, as compared to 6.3 percent in the LaFollette group, and 75 percent had incomes under $2,000, as compared to 31.8 percent in the LaFollette group. The median income for the LaFollette group was nearly $1,000 more than that of all American families.[16]

Values, rather than absolute need, made the women in the LaFollette sample willing to go to work in spite of the relatively high earnings of their husbands. The combination of desirable jobs and a higher standard

Table 4.2.   Income of husbands of 652 gainfully employed women homemakers

Incomes[a] ($)	No. husbands	% distribution
Unemployed	128	19.6
Under 1,000	41	6.3
1,000-1,999	166	25.5
2,000-2,999	138	21.2
3,000-3,999	57	8.7
4,000-4,999	19	2.9
5,000-5,999	9	1.4
6,000-6,999	2	0.3
7,000 and over	8	1.2
Unknown	84	12.9
Total	652	100.0

Source: Cecile Tipton LaFollette, A Study of the Problems of 652 Gainfully Employed Married Women Homemakers, Contributions to Education, no. 619, (New York: Bureau of Publications, Teachers College, Columbia University, 1934), p. 31.

a. Mean income = $2,323; median = $2,094; mode = $1,500.

of living was bringing many women of the middle class into the labor force. But the Women's Bureau continued to stress economic need as the primary motive, without differentiating between absolute and relative need. In 1936 the bureau published a study based upon 1930 census data which summarized the status of the employed woman homemaker.[17] It showed that more than 3.8 million women combined the roles of home-maker and wage-earner in 1930 and that nearly one million of these women were from families with no male head. But only one-eighth of the total number of women, or about 450,000, were the only wage-earners in their families. Not surprisingly, the women tended to be employed in the low-paying, low-prestige occupations, such as domestic and personal service, agriculture, and manufacturing. Practically one-sixth of them, or 164,000, took in lodgers.

The bureau found that gainfully employed homemakers were, on the average, somewhat older than all employed women. A third of them were forty-five years or older. Black women were heavily overrepresented; only about 10 percent of native white and foreign white families, as compared with 40 percent of black families, had a gainfully employed homemaker. Only about 8 percent of all families in the United States with children under ten had a gainfully employed homemaker. In more than 60 percent of these families the woman was in agriculture work, domestic and personal service, or manufacturing.

But the 1930 census data provided little information about family standards of living. The studies of family income and expenditure done by the Bureau of Labor Statistics in 1935-1936 were more helpful in this respect. To cite one example, the Chicago study, which was based on a 10 percent sample of all the families in the city, offered strong evidence that the role of the wage-earning wife was supplemental rather than primary in the great majority of families.[18]

In 14 percent of the native white families of Chicago, a woman was the principal wage-earner, but three-fourths of these families were not complete; that is, they did not have both husband and wife. In the complete families for which information was tabulated, a woman was the principal wage-earner in only 4.3 percent of the cases. In only 2.5 percent of the families was this woman a wife. The wife was the sole wage-earner in less than one percent of the native white complete families. About one-fifth of the native white complete families that reported, or 5,000 out of 25,800, had supplementary wage-earners, and in 26.6 percent of them the supplementary wage-earner was the wife. Over half of the families in which the wife added to the family earnings had less than $2,000 annual income, and 12.2 percent had less than $1,000.[19]

The *Woman Worker*, a monthly publication of the Women's Bureau, in commenting on this study, expressed the view that a family living in a large city at an income level of $1,000 to $2,000 was in definite need of the wife's contribution. But nearly 80 percent of all American families had an income under $2,000, and nearly 42 percent were under $1,000. Among nonrelief families, 57.5 percent were under $2,000 and 22.7 percent were under $1,000.[20] It is apparent that, by the economic standards of 1935-1936, these Chicago women who were performing as supplementary wage-earners were, in many cases, members of middle-income families. Their supplementary wage may have made the difference between a low-income family and a middle-income family, and their reasons for working may have been economic; but their needs were relative, not absolute.

Not all observers followed the Women's Bureau lead in concentrating upon the married woman worker from the low-income family. The National Federation of Business and Professional Women's Clubs conducted a survey in 1937 in response to a request from the International Labor Office for facts on the status of women workers in the United States. The federation's survey covered women white-collar workers in 47 states, Alaska, and Hawaii, and it was particularly concerned with the family circumstances of gainfully employed women. Over 12,000 members of federated clubs responded to the survey, and of these, only 3 percent had contributed nothing to the household in which they lived. The other 97 percent supported themselves, either wholly or partially, and almost half of them, or 48 percent, had other persons partially or totally dependent on them. One-sixth of the group, or 17 percent, were the sole support of households of two to eight persons.[21]

But most of these women were probably better able to afford their responsibilities than the factory or service worker. About 75 percent of them made over $1,000 a year, and the median earning per year was $1,520 for independent workers and $1,310 for salaried workers. Older women tended to have higher earnings, and they were also more likely to be supporting dependents, often their parents rather than children.

Another federation study done in 1939 was directly concerned with the issue of family purchasing power in relation to the work of married women. Ruth Shallcross, who directed the study, differentiated between women who worked because of extreme necessity and those who worked to improve their standard of living. The federation membership represented the second group. They were the women who lived in families with yearly incomes above $1,000, although it may have been their own contributions that raised their incomes above that mark. According to Shallcross, this group performed an important economic function through the consumption of "extras," such as a home in a better neighborhood, household repairs and equipment, household help, and automobiles: "To prevent such women from maintaining their standard of living would merely equalize poverty—would merely curtail drastically their power to buy all products except bare necessities."[22]

Shallcross' analysis reflected a growing recognition on the part of at least some economists and sociologists that not all married working women were from poverty-level homes and that this was not necessarily a bad thing. Early in the Depression, William F. Ogburn had noted the impact of the standard of living upon the number of working women. He pointed out that the desire to improve and maintain a higher standard of living simply increased the difficulty of reaching an adequate level of income for most families and stimulated their desire to raise the standard further by putting the wife to work.[23]

A similar view was expressed by Helen E. Davis of Pi Lambda Theta, who pointed out that society could not insist that woman's place was in the home without guaranteeing an adequate home and something to do in it. With the economic function of the home much reduced, the entire financial burden of supporting should not fall upon the men: "The man is forced to meet greater demands all the time with a dwindling source of supply. The prospect of American homes filled with overworked harassed men and underworked, frustrated women is hardly inviting."[24]

The relationship of economic need to the gainful employment of married women was an issue that could not be resolved because it was a matter of individual interpretation. That is, each family decided for itself at which point it was willing to accept the inconvenience of a working wife and mother in order to achieve a better standard of living. But the investigations of working women that were carried out during the 1920s and 1930s, although sympathetic to the women and their right to work, did not give a balanced interpretation of the economic need of working women in relation to family economics. It is true that most working women were from lower-income families, but it is also true that there was a growing number of married working women from families of a middle-income. The census report of 1940 offered more information on family economics than any previous census; in particular, it contained valuable information on the economic status of working women. These data make it possible to separate from the majority of working women the minority who worked for reasons beyond mere economic survival.

By 1939, American family income had already risen considerably above the standard of 1935-1936. The median family wage or salary income in 1939 was $1,226, or about $200 more than the median income of the earlier survey. This estimate did not take into account total income, which would include profits, rents, or income from other sources. Also, it did not include families who had no wage or salary income and lived entirely on profits, investments, or property. Therefore, it cannot be strictly compared to the earlier study. But wage and salary incomes alone would be somewhat lower than total incomes, since many families had incomes in addition to their wages and salaries, and the self-employed in the business and professional classes had higher incomes than wage-earners and salaried workers. But in 1939, families who were dependent upon a wage or salary already had a higher income than the total incomes of 1935-1936. The middle 40 percent were earning from $800 to $2,000, with almost 11 percent concentrated at the top of that range, earning $1,600 to $2,000.[25]

The labor force participation of married women was related to wage and salary income, as shown by a study of husbands incomes in 1939

(Table 4.3). If not just the husband's income but the entire family's income had been given, the figures would have been higher since they would have included the earnings of other family members as well as the income from all other sources. The figures nevertheless indicate a strong relationship between low income and labor force participation. That is, the women whose husbands were in the lower income groups were overrepresented in the work force. For instance, in metropolitan areas, about 23 percent of all husbands earned under $1,000 a year, but their wives contributed about 33 percent of the female work force. In smaller urban areas, low-income wives were even more heavily overrepresented. This was no doubt because women outside of metropolitan areas had a lower tendency to work. Thus, those who did enter the labor force were more likely to be responding to need rather than opportunity.

The married women also had higher rates of participation at the lower income levels, but the difference was not as great, particularly in the metropolitan areas. About one in four married women worked at the lowest income level, and one in seven worked at the range just under $2,000. The range $2,000 to $2,999 seems to represent a significant change in the tendency to work. But a surprisingly small proportion of women were employed at the low economic levels. One would expect that in all categories under $600, many more women would be employed than actually were. This low employment emphasizes the extent to which married working women were still in a minority at all economic levels. Working involved a question not only of need but also of how that need was defined.

[The earnings of working wives could often lift the family of a low-level wage-earner into the middle class, depending upon how much the women could earn.] In most cases their wages were very low. In 1939, 23 percent of all experienced women in the labor force earned less than $100 and 31.2 percent, or nearly a third, earned less than $200. Another 38.8 percent earned between $200 and $800, and 26.5 percent earned over $800. These figures included part-time workers, occasional workers, and the unemployed, as well as those on public emergency work. No doubt there were many women who worked for a brief stint to cover a short-term emergency or need. But earnings were low even among those who worked a full twelve months: 13.9 percent were still below $100; 18.6 percent were below $200; and only 43.2 percent made more than $800.[26]

Although these earnings sound insignificant, they must be compared to the low wages commanded by the husbands of many of these women. Even a few hundred dollars could make quite a difference in the living

Table 4.3. Income of husbands of women 18-64 years old with husband present, 1939

Wage or salary income ($)	% of wives		% distribution in labor force		Proportion in labor force
Metropolitan areas (100,000 or more)					16.2
Husbands without other income	72.2		74.4		16.7
None or unknown		4.8		7.1	24.3
1-199		1.0		1.7	27.6
200-399		2.6		3.9	24.2
400-599		4.0		5.6	22.7
600-999		11.2		14.8	21.7
1,000-1,499		17.5		20.3	18.8
1,500-1,999		14.6		12.6	14.0
2,000-2,999		11.5		6.5	9.2
3,000 and over		5.00		1.7	5.6
Husband with other income	27.8		25.6		14.9
Urban areas (25,000-100,000)					19.4
Husbands without other income	73.5		76.3		20.2
None or unknown		4.8		7.4	29.9
1-199		1.6		2.8	33.7
200-399		4.5		6.6	28.5
400-599		6.4		9.3	28.0
600-999		14.1		19.1	26.3
1,000-1,499		17.8		17.5	19.2
1,500-1,999		12.2		9.3	14.7
2,000-2,999		8.7		3.6	8.1
3,000 and over		3.4		0.8	4.8
Husband with other income	26.5		23.7		17.4
Urban (2,500-25,000)					18.0
Husband without other income	68.8		71.2		18.6
None or unknown		5.1		7.9	28.1
1-199		2.3		3.7	29.7
200-399		5.7		7.7	24.5
400-599		7.1		8.9	22.5
600-999		14.6		18.4	22.5
1,000-1,499		15.8		15.1	17.1
1,500-1,999		9.7		6.4	11.9
2,000-2,999		6.4		2.5	6.9
3,000 and over		2.1		0.5	4.3
Husband with other income	31.2		28.8		16.9

Source: Sixteenth Census of the United States, 1940. Population: The Labor Force (Sample Statistics) Employment and Family Characteristics of Women (Washington, D.C.: Government Printing Office, 1943), pp. 133-135.

standards of the low-income families. The problem is that there are no figures on earnings by marital status, so there is no way of knowing if married women were making wages comparable to single women. However, there are figures on the wage or salary income of the wife of the household head as related to the husband's income in 1939 (Table 4.4). The most important implication of these incomes is that low-paid women were most often married to low-paid men, and the more a women earned, the less she needed it. The great majority of wage- or salary-earning married women earned very little: 80 percent earned less than $1,000, and over half made less than $600. Moreover, 52.2 percent of the women earning under $200 were married to men earning less than $600. The concentration of married working women in low-income families is striking: over one-third were in families in which the husband made less than $600.

Out of the entire 2.65 million women, however, over one-half, or 56.3 percent, had husbands who made from $600 to $2,000; over a fourth of the husbands earned between $1,200 and $2,000. It was in this broad

Table 4.4. Women workers in urban and rural nonfarm areas at each income level by income level of husband, 1939

Wage or salary ($)	Total	Husband			
		Under $600	$600–$1,199	$1,200–$1,999	$2,000 and over
1-199	19.4	52.2	27.2	16.5	4.1
200-399	18.2	41.4	33.0	20.5	5.1
400-599	15.5	34.8	36.3	23.7	5.2
600-799	16.2	26.2	39.2	28.5	6.1
800-999	10.6	22.5	30.8	37.7	9.0
1,000-1,199	7.1	22.8	22.7	40.0	14.5
1,200-1,399	5.0	23.6	15.7	41.7	19.0
1,400-1,599	3.0	23.0	13.6	37.5	25.9
1,600-1,999	2.6	26.0	10.1	33.7	30.2
2,000 and over	2.4	31.0	7.4	16.4	45.2
Total	100.0	34.6	29.8	26.5	9.1
% of women with wage or salary	15.5	20.9	18.2	13.8	7.3

Source: Sixteenth Census of the United States, 1940. Family Wage or Salary Income (Washington, D.C.: Government Printing Office, 1943), p. 151.

middle range that values rather than need began to influence decisions regarding work. The decision would have been complex, relating to personal family circumstances, such as the number and age of children, the desired standard of living, and the availability of suitable work. But it could not be seen as a case of absolute need. Women in the husband's income range of $600 to $1,199 were almost as likely to work as those in the husband's income range of under $600.

Another way to estimate the economic status of married women workers is to relate employment to occupational grouping and employment status of the husband (Table 4.5). In 1940, women who were married to men in low-paying, low-prestige jobs were more likely to be in the labor force than the wives of men in "middle-class" or white-collar occupations. For instance, over half of the wives of domestic service workers were in the labor force, probably as domestic service workers themselves. Over a fourth of the wives of service workers, excluding domestic and protective, were in the labor force.

But these two groups did not contribute a very large share of the female labor force because there were not many husbands in these occupations. In fact, 55.8 percent of all working wives were married to men who were in the category of proprietors, managers, and officials; clerical and sales workers; craftsmen and foremen; or factory operatives. All but the last of these four categories could be considered middle class, two of them being white-collar and the third being skilled work requiring experience and bestowing a certain amount of prestige. Thus, although women with husbands in low-paying jobs were more likely to be in the labor force, a large proportion of married working women were married to men in "middle-class" occupations. This does not mean that the women themselves were in parallel occupational fields, but it does suggest that the occurrence of working wives was fairly widespread socially, though it still affected only a minority of families in each occupational field. In fact, there was a fairly balanced distribution of working women among the various occupations.

There is no single answer to the question of why women worked during the 1920s and 1930s. A number of related factors have been suggested, including the decline of child labor, the decline in the birth rate, the changing economic function of the home, the availability of desirable jobs, and a potentially higher standard of living. In view of the low incomes of these decades and the rising expectations with respect to standard of living, it is not surprising that married women were entering the labor force. What is surprising is that they remained a small minority. By

Table 4.5. Employment status and occupation of husbands of married women 18-64 years old with husband present, 1940

Employment status and occupation of husband	No. married women with husband present (millions)	No. in labor force (millions)	% in labor force	% distribution
Husband employed (excluding emergency work)	22.3	3.0	13.7	100.0
Professionals, semiprofessionals	1.3	.18	13.7	4.8
Farmers, farm managers	3.8	.17	4.4	4.6
Proprietors, managers, officials	2.6	.40	15.2	11.7
Clerical and sales workers	2.7	.46	17.0	12.5
Craftsmen, foremen	3.76	.47	12.4	12.7
Operatives	4.1	.69	16.8	18.9
Domestic workers	.06	.03	56.4	0.9
Protective service workers	.37	.04	10.9	1.1
Service workers except domestic and protective	.82	.21	25.3	5.6
Farm laborers and foremen	.77	.09	11.6	2.4
Other laborers	1.7	.28	16.3	7.8
Unknown	0.1	.01	14.4	10.5
Husband on emergency work and seeking work	2.8	.38	13.6	10.2
Not in labor force	1.6	.25	15.7	6.8
Total	26.6	3.7	13.8	100.0

Source: Sixteenth Census of the United States, 1940, Employment and Family Characteristics of Women (Washington, D.C.: Government Printing Office, 1943), p. 164.

1940 there were over 4 million married women workers over the age of fourteen, but they still represented only 15 percent of all married women.[27] Even at the lowest income levels, only one in four married women was working. Since the great majority of Americans were living on low incomes during the Depression, the question is not so much why a small minority of married women accepted employment but why such a large majority did not, in spite of the fact that they too experienced unsatisfied economic needs as a result of inadequate wages.

The answer lies partly in the cultural values held by most American families, by the poor as well as by the middle class. One group that did not share the dominant value system, black families, had a much higher proportion than whites of wives and mothers in the labor force at all economic levels. For most white Americans, a working wife placed a stigma upon the husband and the family—a stigma that could not be easily removed but which might be justified by the presence of economic necessity. Also, during the 1930s many women simply did not have job opportunities, particularly those women of lower-income families who were less likely to have skills to sell on the labor market. Unemployment was a reality for women as well as for men, and women had to face the additional problem of job discrimination and hostile public opinion.

Nonetheless, the fact that there was an increase in the number and proportion of married women in the labor force between 1920 and 1940 indicates that traditional values were gradually breaking down in the face of other, more concrete changes. The public discussion of women's roles in the family and in the broader community strongly suggests that an important minority of women and their families were willing to accept a new life-style in response to a personal recognition of economic realities. To the extent that these women were from middle-income families, where they could make choices, they were influenced by values as well as absolute need in their determination to work. This does not contradict the assumption that many, if not most, married women worked because of economic need; but economic need is a relative concept, and it becomes a reality for different families at different levels of experience. Most women could argue that they worked because they had to work, but they defined their needs differently from the nonworking wives whose husbands had similar incomes.

5

Working Women in the Great Depression

The first decades of the twentieth century witnessed a restructuring of the work opportunities available to American women. The economic developments of this period created new jobs in the service and clerical occupations. Because of the important shifts in the occupational characteristics of the female work force, economic distress alone does not explain the impact of the Great Depression upon working women. The bread lines, the labor strikes, the New Deal—all of these were symbols of the 1930s, but none of them really expressed what happened to women workers during these years. Women stood in the bread lines, participated in the strikes, and benefited from the New Deal, but women workers felt the long-range impact of the Depression in a different and less measurable way than men.

In particular, women's movement into white-collar and professional work was retarded, and not only were women unemployed but they were discouraged both materially and psychologically from advancing themselves in the world of work. The antagonism toward the woman worker, which had always been present. even in times of prosperity, was greatly intensified by the Depression, and it had its greatest impact on the white-collar woman worker, especially if she happened to be married.

The developments of the 1930s must be viewed in the context of the long-range trends that affected the occupational characteristics of the female work force. At the turn of the century most working women were employed as domestics, farm laborers, unskilled factory operatives, seamstresses, and teachers. But during the next several decades there was a rapid restructuring of women's work. Two occupational categories—agriculture and manufacturing or mechanical industries—showed a measurable decline, while clerical occupations, trade, and professional services showed a marked increase. The most dramatic shift into these last three fields had occurred by 1920 (Tables 5.1 and 5.2).

Table 5.1. Occupational distribution of female labor force, 1890-1930

Occupation	1890	1900	1910	1920	1930
Agriculture	17.3	18.4	22.4	12.7	8.5
Forestry, fishing	a	a	a	a	a
Mining	a	a	a	a	a
Manufacturing, mechanical industry	27.6	29.9	22.5	22.6	17.5
Transportation, communication	0.3	0.5	1.4	2.6	2.6
Trade	2.4	3.8	5.9	7.9	9.0
Public service	0.1	0.2	0.1	0.1	0.2
Professional service	7.9	8.0	9.1	11.9	14.2
Domestic and personal service	41.2	37.1	31.3	25.6	29.6
Clerical work	3.1	5.1	7.3	16.6	18.5

Source: H. Dewey Anderson and Percy E. Davidson, *Occupational Trends in the United States* (California: Stanford University Press, 1940), p. 19; *Fifteenth Census of the United States, 1930. Population,* vol. V, *General Report on Occupations* (Washington, D.C.: Government Printing Office, 1933), p. 39.
a. Less than .01 precent.

Table 5.2. Occupational distribution of female labor force, 1940

Occupation	% distribution
Professionals, semiprofessionals	12.3
Proprietors, managers, officials, including farmers	4.7
Clerical and sales workers	27.9
Craftsmen, foremen	1.0
Operatives	19.2
Protective service workers	a
Service workers except protective	28.9
Laborers, including farm laborers	3.7
Unknown	2.3

Source: Sixteenth Census of the United States, 1940. Vol. III, *The Labor Force,* Pt. I, *U.S. Summary* (Washington, D.C.: Government Printing Office, 1943), p. 87.

The new occupational pattern paralleled a number of long-term trends in the American economy. The decline of agriculture is perhaps the most self-evident, although the really significant decline for women workers in this field came between 1910 and 1920 rather than earlier. In 1910 the percentage of working women in agriculture actually increased over the previous decades (Appendix D). But by 1920 it had become clear that agriculture was no longer an important area of employment for women. Manufacturing too became less important for women as heavy industry began to dominate industrial production between 1880 and 1910. Even as early as the 1840s native-born women factory workers were being replaced by immigrant men and women in unskilled work. At the same time a solidification of barriers against women in skilled factory work prevented their upward mobility. Certain kinds of light industry, such as food processing and clothing, continued to employ numbers of women, but by the late nineteenth century, immigrant women were predominant over native-born women in factory work.[1]

Since women were not entering the expanding sector of industrial employment, a pool of female workers became available to meet the demands of an economy that was becoming rapidly bureaucratized. The development of the corporate form of business, the emergence of America as a major industrial and trade power, and the rapid urbanization of the country expanded the need for communication and record keeping. The demand for clerical workers grew so rapidly from the 1890s and throughout the twentieth century that it could not have been met if employers had been unwilling to hire women. Then, too, women could be hired more cheaply than men, and very soon they began to fulfill specialized roles within the office hierarchy.[2]

The movement into clerical work, trade, and professional services partially obscured the fact that right through the 1930s, nearly 30 percent of all working women were in domestic and personal service. But the nature of that occupational category was also changing. Many of the women worked as hairdressers and manicurists, midwives and practical nurses, and elevator tenders. The service category also included employees, owners, and managers of steam laundries, attendants in hospitals or other large institutions, and hotel or restaurant keepers. In view of the definitional extent of the category, it is not surprising that gains were made in the 1920s that reversed the trend of earlier decades.[3]

In spite of the large number of women in service occupations, the overall trend in the social-economic status of the female labor force during the first part of the twentieth century was definitely upward. A Women's

Bureau study which divided women into socioeconomic groups illustrates the shift in distribution over a thirty-year period. The study found that the change within ten socioeconomic groups was most marked in the white-collar occupations. Women clerks and kindred workers had been the fourth largest group in 1910, but by 1940 they constituted the largest group. Within the broad category of clerical occupations, "office workers" were the most numerous and the most important field for women. The term "office workers" in 1940 included stenographers, typists, and secretaries; shipping and receiving clerks; clerical and kindred workers; and office machine operators. Important numbers of women also worked in other white-collar categories as bookkeepers, accountants, cashiers, and telephone operators.[4]

The other important white-collar field that opened its doors to women during these years was sales. In particular women tended to concentrate in the occupations of salespersons and demonstrators. Real estate selling also became important, for although the actual numbers involved were not great, women made significant gains in proportion to men. By 1940 there were over 40,000 women in real estate, and they represented 20 percent of all real estate workers, whereas in 1910 there had been only 3,000 women real estate workers, or about 2 percent of the total number of workers in this occupation.[5]

The gains made in the professions were not extensive: 9.2 percent of all working women in 1910 were professionals, as compared to 12.2 percent in 1940. But women were actually overrepresented in the professional fields in proportion to their numbers in the labor force. Throughout the period from 1920 to 1940 women constituted nearly half of all professionals. However, this proportional representation is a deceptive guide to status, for women were concentrated in two major low-status professions, teaching and nursing, and they heavily dominated a number of other fields, such as social work, library science, and religious work. By contrast, they made few significant inroads into the more prestigious professions, such as law, medicine, architecture, and engineering.[6]

The concentration of women in a few of the professions was a reflection of the employment pattern that prevailed in all of the major occupational fields. Even as new economic opportunities emerged for both men and women, certain kinds of jobs were implicitly labeled for one sex or the other. All societies have had a division of labor based upon sex, although the same kinds of work have not been designated male or female in all societies. Generally rationale for this sex differentiation has been related to economic subsistence, the maintenance of social order, or religious belief. In America the terms "women's work" and "a man's job" have always been value-laden expressions which carried over into domestic and personal roles as well as economic functions. Occupations such as domestic service, nursing, and teaching were obvious extensions of the traditional "women's work." Similarly, when women moved into factory work, they filled jobs that were closely related to their past production of food and clothing. Even the clerical positions fit the pattern of male dominance and female service, since the women were expected to play a supportive role to the men who did the important work of the world.

This division of labor based on sex roles limited the economic opportunities of both men and women, but it was particularly detrimental to women's social and economic status because they were limited in their access to high-status work. The division also presented an easy and effective means of keeping women's wages down. Since "women's work" was by definition low-status, women were paid less than their male counterparts. This distinction held even when women were doing the same work as men.[7]

But there is another side to this pattern of work segregation. The fact that certain jobs were reserved for women meant that there was always a market for female labor. If most women workers had been widely scattered throughout the occupational system, so that the sexes were readily interchangeable, then it would not have made much sense to talk about a demand for female labor. But since a fairly high proportion of all female workers were concentrated in predominantly female occupations, then the demand for workers in these occupations created a demand for female labor. Thus men and women seldom competed in the same labor market, even during a period of depression.[8]

The sex segregation of the labor force contributed to the movement of women away from manual labor and into white-collar occupations during the years from 1910 to 1940 (Table 5.3 and Appendix E). Several other significant developments are revealed by the figures for this period. First of all, domestic and personal service held its own during the thirty-year period, declining almost not at all. Although laborers and semi-skilled operatives declined considerably, the most abrupt decreases came before 1930; there was very little change during the 1930s. The white-collar occupations gained considerably over the years; but once again, most of the gains were made before 1930, and the decade between 1910 and 1920 was the most significant. The 1930s showed almost no gain at all.

Table 5.3.   Distribution of female labor force by type of work

| Year | White collar | | Domestic and personal services | | Laborers and Semi-skilled operatives | |
	%	Millions	%	Millions	%	Millions
1910	23.3	1.8	31.3	2.4	45.4	3.5
1920	38.5	3.2	25.6	2.1	35.8	3.0
1930	44.0	4.7	29.6	3.1	26.5	2.8
1940	44.9	5.7	28.9	3.7	23.9	3.0

Source: Tables 5.1 and 5.2.

Between 1910 and 1940 the white-collar field and the manual labor field exactly reversed positions. This structural change came at a time when the female labor force was not expanding proportionally, but its marital characteristic was changing as more married women went to work. Married women were much less likely to be employed in white-collar occupations than were single women. But during the 1920s they were moving into these fields at a more rapid rate than that of the female working force as a whole. According to a rough estimate, in 1920 21.5 percent of all gainfully employed married women were engaged in white-collar work, and in 1930 the figure was 32.5 percent, or an impressive 51.2 percent rate of increase. The female work force as a whole saw only a 13 percent rate of increase in white-collar work during the same decade.[9]

But the Depression of the 1930s had a negative overall effect on working women, particularly with respect to their occupational status. Although it may be disputed whether the twentieth-century shift in the occupational structure for women represented an actual advancement for them as individuals, it seems clear that most women saw white-collar work as a standard of occupational and social mobility.[10] During the 1930s there was a definite decline in this kind of mobility, as shown by data from the 1910 through 1940 census reports on the rate of change in the percentage of female workers in three broad occupational categories: white-collar, service, and laboring or semiskilled work (Table 5.4). Although the rate of movement into each of these categories declined somewhat during the 1930s, the reasons were different in each case. The decline in the rate of movement into manufacturing and industry was part of a long-term trend away from manual and unskilled labor, which actu-

Table 5.4. Change in distribution of female labor force, 1910-1940

Year	White-collar		Domestic and personal services		Laborers and semiskilled operatives	
	% distr.	Change rate	% distr.	Change rate	% distr.	Change rate
1910	23.5	—	31.3	—	45.2	—
1920	38.6	+64.3	25.6	−18.2	35.8	−20.8
1930	44.0	+14.0	29.6	+15.6	26.5	−26.0
1940[a]	44.9	+2.1	28.9	−2.4	23.9	−9.8

Source: Anderson and Davidson, *Occupational Trends in the United States,* p. 19; *Fifteenth Census of the United States: 1930. Population,* vol. V, *General Report on Occupations* (Washington, D.C.: Government Printing Office, 1933), p. 39; *Sixteenth Census of the United States, 1940.* Vol. III, *The Labor Force,* Pt. I, *U.S. Summary* (Washington, D.C.: Government Printing Office, 1943), p. 87.

a. The 1940 figures total only 97.7% because 2.3% of all working women did not report an occupation.

ally slowed down during the Depression. The category of domestic and personal service is a special case, since it covers such a wide range of occupations. No doubt women in industry and in domestic or personal service suffered more severely in material terms than white-collar workers during the Depression. But the decline in the rate of movement into white-collar and professional work best illustrated the impact of the Depression upon women's occupational status.

The rate of movement into white-collar work had already begun to drop in the 1920s, probably as part of a natural slowing-down process after years of unusually rapid growth. Moreover, the movement of more married women into the labor force had a somewhat negative effect upon the occupational pattern, since married women were more likely to be concentrated in low-status work (Table 5.5). Women's relatively slow occupational progress after 1920 was also due in part to the rapid expansion of fields in which women were underrepresented, such as the scientific professions, college teaching, and high-paying managerial occupations.[11] But while all of these factors had a bearing upon occupational distribution for women in the 1930s, the evidence indicates that the twin burdens of unemployment and economic discrimination during the Depression most hindered individual advancement and retarded the occupational mobility of women as a group.

Table 5.5.   Married women workers over 14 years old, 1910-1940

Year	% gainfully occupied	Rate of increase	% of female labor force	Rate of increase
1910	10.7	—	24.7	—
1920	9.0	−15.9	23.0	−6.7
1930	11.7	+30.0	28.9	+25.7
1940	15.3	+30.8	35.5	+22.8

Source: Bancroft, The American Labor Force, p. 45.

The most obvious factor limiting the opportunities of all American workers was the problem of unemployment. Throughout the Depression the proportion of unemployed women was smaller than that of unemployed men, although this situation varied from year to year as well as from place to place. In the early years of the Depression, women seeking work had several advantages over men. In particular, they were likely to work more cheaply, simply because women workers had always been paid less than men. Also, much of women's work, such as domestic service, secretarial or clerical work, and some kinds of factory work, was so stereotyped that it was virtually closed to men. Furthermore, women's attitudes toward work were sometimes more flexible than men's, particularly if they were forced to work because of the unusual circumstances of the Depression. They were likely to see their plight as a temporary aberration rather than a permanent condition.[12]

Perhaps a more obvious reason for the relatively low unemployment rate for women was that offered by Margaret H. Hogg, an economist who surveyed a group of families in New Haven, Connecticut, in 1931. She noted that women tended to drop out of the labor market when work was unobtainable. That is, rather than viewing themselves as an unemployed part of the labor force, they viewed themselves in terms of their traditional nonworking role. Thus, it is possible that there were many women who did not appear in the unemployment statistics but who might well have accepted a job had one been available.[13]

In spite of a relatively lower unemployment rate, women were nonetheless directly and severely affected by the Depression. In 1937 an enumerative check was conducted as part of the census which estimated that there were over 3 million totally unemployed women workers in November of that year; the total female labor force in the 1930s was about 11 million. An additional 398,000 women were estimated to be working on WPA and other emergency jobs, making a total of about 3.5 million women without normal employment. Another 1.5 million had intermittent or part-time employment. Throughout most of the 1930s women in domestic and personal service carried the burden of unemployment in proportionately greater numbers than women in other fields, according to a 1937 Women's Bureau study of women in particular occupations who were seeking employment.[14] In the case of professional women and salespeople, unemployment rates were relatively low, but not all white-collar workers fared as well. The second highest percentage of women seeking work was in the clerical occupations.

Clerical work had long been the goal of young lower-middle-class women who had to earn their livings, as well as that of large numbers of other young women who merely wanted to work for a few years before marriage. But by the 1930s the field no longer offered the wide-open opportunities for employment that had been characteristic of previous decades. Almost every good-sized American city during these years had its business school, tempting patrons with slogans such as "Take our six months' course and prepare yourself for a career" or "Positions guaranteed to all graduates." But the guarantee became increasingly hard to make good. Depression conditions lessened the need for clerical workers, and the situation was exacerbated by the fact that in many cities the only public-school trade course open to women was the high school "commercial course.[15]

A special census of unemployment in Massachusetts in 1934 reported nearly 9,500 young women who were vocationally trained but had never worked. Of this number, 7,500 were trained for clerical work. A Women's Bureau study pointed out that in New Bedford, Massachusetts, 663 girls were enrolled in commercial courses in 1934-1935, but only 34 members of the June 1934 graduating class were placed in clerical positions. A report of the United States Employment Service showed 177,000 women seeking clerical work in November 1937, but only 5,300 were placed in such jobs, and half of these positions were temporary.[16]

Temporary and part-time work was often the only work available to women who desperately needed a job. Thus the unemployment figures understated the economic straits of many working women who, although listed as employed, were actually underemployed. Saleswomen were typical in this respect. Many of them worked part-time during the peak hours of business. For some women, particularly married women, this was a convenient arrangement. But for others who needed full-time employment, the job was taken simply because there was no full-time work to be had.

Saleswomen also faced total unemployment. In November 1937, nearly 58,000 women were registered for sales positions with the United States Employment Service, but only 4,800 were placed, and well over half of these were in temporary jobs. Data on the employment of women in stores varied from state to state, but in general, by 1935 the level of employment was above the low point of 1929. And as Table 5.6 indicates, saleswomen did not have the high unemployment rates of other occupational groups, perhaps because of the fact that many were underemployed.[17]

Professional women also had low unemployment rates in comparison to other occupational groups, but the case of the professional worker requires special attention, for the statistical evidence probably understated the impact of unemployment to a greater extent than was true for any other occupational group. For one thing, professional women often possessed sufficient skills to enable them to move into other occupations, so that whereas they were not actually unemployed, they were probably not working in the job of choice and might well have experienced a loss of status.[18] Also, professional women were often able simply to drop out of the labor market when work was not available to them, either because they were married to men with professional positions, or because they had other family support. This is not to suggest that all professional

Table 5.6. Women workers seeking employment by occupation, July 1936

Normally employed (1930)	% distr.	Seeking employment (1936)	% distr.
Domestic and personal Service	29.6	Service work	50.9
Clerical work	18.5	Clerical work	15.5
		Manufacturing,	
Professional service	14.2	mechanical industry	10.8
Trade	9.0	Sales work	4.8
Other	11.2	Other	12.3
Total	100.0	Total	100.0

Source: Mary E. Pidgeon, Women in the Economy of the United States: A Summary Report, U.S. Department of Labor, Women's Bureau, Bulletin no. 155 (Washington, D.C.: Government Printing Office, 1937), p. 37.

women in the 1930s were financially independent apart from their work. Nonetheless, they were more likely to have family resources to fall back upon, and they were more likely than was the average woman worker to be working for reasons other than strictly economic need.

In 1934, Lorine Pruette did a study of employment and unemployment among the members of the American Woman's Association. This organization had a membership of 4,000 women, more than 75 percent of whom were actively engaged in a business or profession. The association was not representative of the country as a whole, since about 90 percent of the membership lived in New York City or within a ninety-mile radius of the city. But the study nonetheless suggested the extent to which professional and business women were affected by the Depression. Although the association's members were in a very favorable position compared to working women as a whole, during the three years covered by the survey, unemployment was a reality at one time or another for 29 percent of those responding to the questionnaire. The evidence that Pruette compiled indicated that even temporary unemployment resulted in a loss of professional status. Re-employment did not guarantee a return to former status. Even during the affluent years of earlier decades, professional women had to be better than their male competition when applying for good jobs. With the tightening up of the job market, women were more likely to be pushed down into lower occupational levels.[19]

In addition to the loss of occupational status there was an obvious loss of money. On the average, these unemployed women lost 16 months out of a possible working period of 56 months. Seventy-five percent were unemployed for at least three months, and almost 10 percent were out of work for at least 36 months. The longest average duration was 22 months, reported by 25 women who were unemployed at the end and the beginning of the period, with some employment in between. The shortest average of unemployment, or 9.7 months, was found among women who were employed at the beginning and end of the period but not by the same organization. Such extended periods of unemployment resulted in considerable financial loss for the women involved. But there was also the matter of declining salaries with which to contend. Over 60 percent of the women reported a salary decrease between 1929 and 1933, although the amounts of the decrease were not reported, so that there is no way of knowing if they exceeded the decline in the cost of living during these years. Also, the general feeling of insecurity, which was present even among those who had not been unemployed or lost earnings, led the overwhelming majority of these women, or 97.7 percent, to cut their budgets.[20]

Perhaps the most important effect that the Depression had upon professional women was that it undermined their self-confidence and forced them to readjust their career aspirations, which was a particularly tragic development since for many of them their careers were their main interest in life. The majority of them were not married, and as Pruette pointed out, they were of the generation that had stressed the importance of jobs and exulted in their own economic independence. They were very proud and thus were not likely to advertise their insecurity nor their economic need: "We shall probably never know the humiliation and disruptive shifts that educated women have resorted to in order to hide their economic distress . . . And to recall that these are the women who by their age and training and marital status largely belong to the women who have sought major satisfactions in their jobs, renouncing marriage and working years to reach their vocational achievements."[21]

Although it is apparent that professional and business women did not suffer to the same extent as other classes of women workers during the Depression, the economic hardships which they faced discouraged and retarded the expansion of their occupational fields. Furthermore, business and professional women, along with other white-collar working women, did not receive the same support and encouragement from the New Deal legislation, which substantially advanced the interests of other classes of women workers. New Deal labor legislation left out large groups of women workers at the bottom and at the top of the economic ladder. For instance, the Fair Labor Standards Act specifically exempted from its provisions many job categories, such as domestic service. The National Recovery Act (NRA) codes applied only to industries in or affecting interstate and foreign commerce, and they covered only about half of all employed women—mainly those in manufacturing, trade, communication, clerical work, and certain large service groups. Many women who were not covered by the codes were working in occupations in which the worst employment conditions prevailed, the most obvious example being that of household employment. Other groups of a similarly low status were also excluded from code provisions. They included laundresses not employed in laundries, dressmakers and seamstresses not working in factories, and women in agriculture and public service.

At the other end of the occupational spectrum were the 1.5 million women in professional service who were also neglected in the NRA codes. And clerical workers received only limited benefit from the codes. Though many of them were technically covered, most of these were located in industries where they received very little benefit, and some clerical workers were not covered at all. Codes were not approved for telephone companies, in which there were more than 235,000 women, nor for insurance companies, where about 150,000 women worked.[22] In general, although clerical workers made a much higher weekly wage than workers in production or service, their hours and working conditions were not as favorable as the public impression of them. A typical work week was forty-four hours, and the clerical worker might be paid anywhere from $15 to $25, depending upon the type of office and its regional location. But most important was the unemployment of office workers during the 1930s, a problem that might have been partially met by unionization, unemployment benefits, and government programs, had there been support for these approaches.

White-collar and professional workers also failed to benefit from Section 7 (a) of the National Industrial Relations Act (NIRA), the provision that revitalized the labor movement for workers in industry by protecting the rights of unions to organize free of employer interference. Thus, the formation of the Committee for Industrial Organization in 1935 marked another advance for the industrial woman worker that was not extended either to the domestic and service worker or to the business and professional woman.[23]

The emergency public employment programs, administered and financed by the federal government, were of little help to white-collar and professional women workers. Women did not participate in the work relief programs to the same degree as men, partly because these programs were aimed at the male breadwinner as the mainstay of family life in America. Furthermore, of the 372,000 women employed on the WPA, more than half of them, or 211,700, worked on projects that emphasized menial domestic work. Thus, garments and supplies made by these women were distributed to relief clients and to hospitals and other public institutions; preserved, canned, and dried surplus food, also produced by them, went to needy families and for school lunch projects.[24]

Many of the women involved in work relief under WPA were in a special program set up in July 1937, called the Household Service Demonstration Project. The program provided training for women who were seeking domestic employment, but it also provided for the employment of women who acted as teachers and demonstrators in the courses. Some 1,700 women were involved in giving a two-month training course, later extended to three months, in methods of cooking and serving food, caring for the house, caring for children, washing, ironing, and marketing. The WPA also employed another 30,000 women on housekeeping-aid projects. Women who were good homemakers but had no other skills were sent into the homes of needy families to help out in times of illness or other distress. In addition, during the 1937-1938 school season, 8,000 women were employed on school lunch projects.[25]

All of these tasks were a reflection of women's traditional domestic roles. None of them really developed skills that could be transferred to other sectors of the labor force. However, women were also employed in the various professional and white-collar projects of the WPA. In fact, although in general not as many women participated in these projects as did men—only 17.5 percent of all WPA workers being female, at a time when women made up about 24 percent of the total labor force—their occupational distribution was much more favorable than was that of their male counterparts. That is, women on WPA projects were more likely to be placed in a white-collar occupation than were men. Nearly one-third of all women working on WPA projects were employed as clerical workers, professional and technical workers, or project supervisors and foremen.[26] One reason for this relatively strong representation in white-collar work was that a high proportion of women in the actual work force were in white-collar occupations. Therefore, it was logical that they were well represented among those seeking work in government-founded projects.

As late as 1940 there were still 1,250,000 women seeking work, and another 450,000 women were employed on public emergency work. Along with unemployment, women workers had to face the additional obstacle of prejudice and discrimination on the part of their prospective employers and co-workers. The antagonism toward the woman worker, which had always been present, even in times of prosperity, was greatly intensified by the Depression. Its most severe impact was felt by the white-collar woman worker, especially if she happened to be married.

The basic argument that emerged during the Depression was that women workers were taking jobs away from unemployed male workers. Actually, this was not usually the case. In direct response to the theory that the entrance of women into gainful occupations had displaced men, the National Industrial Conference Board published a study in 1936, entitled *Women Workers and Labor Supply*, which concluded that there was little evidence that female workers were substituting for male workers, or that women were encroaching upon male occupations. Instead, the increase in women workers during the twentieth century resulted from the fact that the male population of working age was not large enough to supply the labor force needed for new service occupations or to meet the expansion of old ones. Most of the increase in the number of women gainfully employed took place in the distribution and service occupations. Meanwhile, the proportion of women workers in the production industries, particularly in the manufacturing and mechanical industries, was definitely on the decline.[27]

A corollary to the theory that women were displacing men was the assumption that most women did not really have to work because they had someone to support them, and they were therefore working only for "pin money." This issue became the basis for a full-fledged debate over working women during the Depression.[28]

Although the dispute over women's right to work was bound to have a negative effect upon women's attitude toward their role in the world of work, the overall effect was not entirely negative. The interest in women workers resulted in the collection and interpretation of a great deal of data concerning the economic status of women, which brought about an increased awareness of women's economic role. Still, the attitudes expressed were manifestations of a climate of opinion that must have had an impact upon women workers, immeasurable though that impact may be. [Although for the great majority of women who had to work for their economic sustenance, a debate among economists, business leaders, and social workers was of little direct concern, it nevertheless narrowed their opportunities on the job market and directly affected their wages.] Even the NRA codes reflected the general view that women needed less money than men. By September 1, 1934, when 233 NRA codes had been approved, 135 of these codes fixed the minimum rates for women in some forms of production work lower than the rates for men. For example, in three codes women's wage rates were 6.3 percent below men's. This was the smallest difference found. The greatest difference was 30 percent, found in one code. In eighteen codes the difference was less than 10 percent, and in twenty-five codes the difference was 20 percent or more.[29]

Most women working in production or in other unskilled or semi-skilled occupations had little choice in their economic roles. But for those women who were in a position to make decisions regarding their career, the hostile environment of the 1930s was undoubtedly discouraging. This was especially true for married women wishing to pursue a career or simply to work to raise their family's standard of living. [For although all women workers were suspect, outright discrimination through the actions and policies of employers was always directed at the married woman worker.] Direct discriminatory action was thus the logical extension of the "pin-money theory," and the married woman worker, who presumably had a husband to support her, was the natural victim.

Private employers, particularly those in large service industries, and state and federal governmental agencies were the most likely to adopt policies discriminating against the married woman worker. The New England Telephone and Telegraph Company discharged married women in January 1931, and the Northern Pacific Railroad Company followed suit exactly nine months later. Public schoolteachers were often subject to quick dismissal if they were married. The National Education Association made a survey of 1,500 cities in 1930-1931 and found that in 63 percent of the cities a woman teacher was dismissed as soon as she married. Seventy-seven percent of them did not employ married women as new teachers.[30]

Legislative attempts to restrict the employment of married women were plentiful but not particularly successful. However, as the Depression wore on, efforts along these lines intensified. The National Federation of Business and Professional Women's Clubs reported in 1940 that bills directed against married women workers had been introduced in the legislatures of twenty-six states during the previous few years. The bills differed in content, but their intent was obvious: to keep the middle-class married woman out of the job market. Some bills would have barred the married woman only if her husband earned a certain amount, such as $100 a month, or $1,200 or $1,500 a year. But in one state the amount was set at $800 a year, although the WPA study of the cost of living reported that $1,243 was the minimum for family maintenance in a city of that state.[31]

The federal government took more direct discriminatory action than did the state governments. On June 30, 1932, Congress passed the Federal Economy Act which stipulated that no two persons in any family could be employed in government service. The language used in the bill applied to "persons" rather than "women" as such, and theoretically it was anti-nepotistic rather than discriminatory, but in application it discriminated against women. Before the act was repealed in January 1935, 1,603 employees had been discharged; three-fourths of them were women.[32]

Although public sentiment in general was opposed to the married woman worker in business and the professions, particularly during the Depression, in the end the private employer made the hiring and firing decisions. Private policymakers had three considerations to balance: public sentiment as expressed through the attitudes of customers and clients; the simple economics of running a business in terms of efficiency and labor supply; and the private feelings of the individual employer. Often a conservative conscience led a male employer to believe that he was undermining family life by hiring wives and mothers. Also, the over-supply of applicants for the job, and the fact that many of these applicants were totally dependent upon their jobs for a livelihood, caused him to underestimate or deprecate the needs of the married woman who seemingly had a husband to support her.

A study published in 1939 by the National Industrial Conference Board showed that most private employers considered merit more important than marital status, but at the same time they were influenced to some extent by the prevailing opinion that the unemployment would be resolved if married women left the labor market. The general practice was to maintain a flexible policy, with a preference for single women. Practically three-fourths of the companies said that they had no definite, fixed policy concerning women factory employees who married, and 60 percent had no such policy regarding their office employees. Discrimination varied in intensity depending upon the type of office work. For example, 84 percent of the insurance companies, 65 percent of the banks, and 63 percent of the public utilities had restrictions against the employment of married women in their offices, but only 14 percent of the manufacturing concerns and 11 percent of the mercantile establishments had such restrictions against office workers. There was also a wide variation from city to city across the nation, depending on which type of industry predominated.[33]

Sales work was another area of white-collar employment that attracted a particularly high proportion of married women workers. In 1920, 21.1 percent of all saleswomen were married, and in 1930 the proportion was up to 33.5 percent. By 1940, 42.7 percent were married.[34] The National Federation of Business and Professional Women's Clubs made a survey early in 1930 which revealed that only a very small number of department stores refused employment to married women. However, in 1939 the *Department Store Economist* had reported that the sentiment against married women was growing strong. Opposition came from customers, labor organizations, women's clubs, and miscellaneous groups of the unemployed. Despite this opposition, most department store managers were not eager to announce an official policy against hiring or retaining married women. Their hesitancy was partly a matter of public relations and partly a matter of simple economics. Married women's employment was advantageous to department stores because the necessary part-time arrangements were convenient for both parties.[35] [In the end, convenience and efficiency were more important to these employers than the doubtful and debatable principles espoused by those who opposed the married woman's right to work.]

Despite the fact that policies varied widely according to locale, type of industry, and attitude of the employer, married women workers, who had always met with a certain amount of hostility, faced the double burden of job shortage and intensified discrimination during the Depression. Single women perhaps faced less direct discrimination, but they certainly were not presented with the opportunities for responsibility and advancement that most of their male colleagues took for granted. The damage that must have been done to this generation of women can never be measured. Perhaps Pruette came closest to the truth when she speculated that the achievements reached by women in the earlier decades of the century might stand as the high-water mark for many years to come. For the Depression had an impact not only upon the mature women who learned to settle for less but also upon the young women who had never known more: "The lost generation of girls has been marking time in a world that allowed them neither security nor opportunity. They have not had to confront the earlier feminist choice of career versus home of their own for many of them had a chance at neither."[36]

Recent interpretations of American women during the interwar years suggest that this was a period of stagnation—politically, socially, and economically. Moreover, they often place the responsibility for this decline of feminism, of social activism, and of careerism on American women themselves. The feminists were split into factions, and the social reformers spent more time battling the radical feminists over the Equal Rights Amendment than they did reforming. Both groups failed to rally the support of the great mass of women, who lacked the commitment of their forebears and who adopted the materialistic values of the 1920s and the security-oriented values of the 1930s.[37]

Yet given the social and economic obstacles that they faced, many women had little other choice than to retreat from the challenges of an earlier generation and to seek security in the home and family. [And in spite of the relative decline in the occupational status of women during these years, the Depression experience established certain facts. For instance, by the 1930s, women were in the labor market to stay, no matter what the economic conditions or the state of public opinion.] This fact was an inevitable response to long-range changes in the American economic structure which created a demand for female labor; women met this demand because their own needs could no longer be met through work in the home.

[More surprising, perhaps, was the staying power of married women workers as a group. In spite of the overt prejudice and blatant discrimination, married women increased their work force participation both absolutely and proportionately. Perhaps it was a matter of how they sought security, for at a time when men at all economic levels were insecure in their jobs, within the family, at least, there was a gradual acceptance of the working wife as an alternative means to security.[38]

[Finally, the changing economic basis of family life in the twentieth century from a unit of production to one that emphasized consumption meant that the male wage-earner was not always able to support his several family members, in spite of the efforts of reformers, economists, and labor unions. Additional wage-earners have always been important to the American family, and with the decline of child labor in the 1920s and 1930s this responsibility often fell upon the married woman. Thus, the woman worker, both married and single, could hold dear the values of family life, security, and material comfort while at the same time moving into the labor market to protect those values.]

The experience of women in the Depression was discouraging, but it was not a complete reversal of the long-term trends affecting their lives that had emerged with the industrialization of the nation. The women who overcame the economic handicaps and discriminatory policies of the Depression to remain in the work force were never a majority of all American women, but they provided a pattern of combining work and family roles that was to predominate in the post World War II years. [The life-styles adopted by working women continued to be based on traditional family values. The women who worked were doing so in response to their understanding of family need. Although they carried their economic role beyond the confines of their home, the relationship between home, self, and job remained constant. In particular, the work of the married woman usually reflected the primacy of the home life. She was working to pay for a home, keep her children in school, help her husband with his business, or pay for the "extras." It would be a mistake, however, to assume that her home life remained unchanged. The question of the working wife's role and status within the family, and the extent to which these evolved in response to the economic conditions of the Depression, is an issue that must be examined in order to understand the real impact of the 1930s upon American women.

6

Women's Place in the Home

Quantitative trends of American economic life between the world wars can be measured, including the economics of family life, the movement of married women into the work force, the shift in their occupational distribution, and their contributions to family support. But the effects of these developments upon the qualitative aspects of women's lives are more difficult to determine. Sociological studies of family life that were made in the years during and after the Great Depression shed light on two separate but related developments, the employment of women and the economic crisis of the 1930s, as well as on the effect of these developments upon women's role in the family.

[One of the most common ways of explaining the changing nature of family life in the twentieth century is to note the emergence of the "companionship" marriage, in contrast to the patriarchal system of the nineteenth century.] Marriage is by its very nature a partnership, but companionship marriage moves beyond a functional partnership with a sharp division of spheres and an emphasis on the man as patriarch, to a sharing of activities and mutual interests that includes not only work and domestic chores but also recreational and leisure-time concerns. The companionship marriage is not necessarily egalitarian. There may be a dominant partner, but this arrangement is basically satisfactory to both partners because the dominance is defined by them as part of the relationship, rather than forced upon them by tradition.

Many of the studies on this marital arrangement that appeared in the 1950s and 1960s advanced the proposition that men had lost authority with the decline of the patriarchal family and that women had moved into a position of nearly equal partnership.[1] But in recent years, sociologists have questioned this assumption. They argue that most marriages are husband-dominant and that, when the wife obtains more power, it is by default.[2] The 1920s and 1930s were a time of transition in family relations, especially with respect to the economic conditions of those years, and their impact on the position of women in the family. The years are important as they relate not only to the long-term developments of family life but also to women's attitudes toward themselves, their families, and their status in society. The decline of feminism as an ideological and political movement can perhaps be attributed to women's sense that they were making gains in their personal lives, so their interest in ideological feminism lessened.

It has been commonly assumed with respect to women's economic role in the twentieth century that the working wife gains influence in the family and that she may even threaten the husband in his role as head of the house. Much of the popular literature of the 1920s and 1930s, for instance, expressed a concern that the working wife was usurping the authority and prestige of the male provider. Yet the extent to which this was an actual problem is questionable.

In the first place, the new economic opportunities of the twentieth century gave young women a different attitude toward marriage. They were still eager to marry and settle down; but if they had a job, especially a desirable job, their bargaining position on the marriage market was strengthened.[3] As Frances Donovan observed, the saleswoman, for example, was influenced in her attitude toward marriage by the comforting knowledge that she did not have to get married. She was economically independent and could, therefore, make a careful decision when a suitor presented himself.[4]

But as William O'Neill has pointed out, many women expected marriage to be the principal event in their lifetime, leading them to fuller, richer lives. The "modern" woman, whether in school or on the job, saw marriage as an opportunity for sharing joys and sorrows with a man who was more than a mere protector and provider: "The modern union of man and woman is visioned as a perfect consummation of both personalities that will involve every phase of mutual living."[5]

The companionship marriage may have been an expectation for many, but it was not always a reality. Certainly it was more likely to be realized if the two partners approached the relationship from positions of near equality in terms of economic independence. And it was more likely to be upheld if the woman could continue her economic role. But these conditions were rare, and it is also doubtful that they guaranteed an equal partnership. Dair L. Gillespie argued that in the early 1970s there was still a caste/class system supporting the preponderance of the male sex. In the competition for power, the husband had most of the advantages because his contribution to family life had a higher value in the money economy. The wife's participation in the work force could erode the power of the husband, but since she was handicapped by her domestic role, she could seldom compete with her husband in the economic sphere.[6]

According to Margaret M. Poloma and T. Neal Garland, in the early 1970s the balance of power in the family was still determined by more than economics. Few women were inclined to distrub the traditional relationship. Rather, they were constrained by their own concept of the ideal feminine role. They were so concerned about a possible infringement upon their husband's provider role that they were unwilling or unable to relinquish their traditional role.[7]

It is possible that working wives of the 1920s and 1930s were even less likely to intrude upon their husbands' masculine domain. At least there is no evidence to suggest otherwise. Most women saw their work not as a means of increasing their familial role but as a way of maintaining their family economically. Even those few women who were working to satisfy career ambitions rather than family need still undertook the major responsibility for home and child care.

Virginia M. Collier, in a study of 100 married professional women in the mid-1920s, discovered that most of them had servants; only nine did not. Over half of the husbands, or 56, helped with the home and family. They cooked dinner, washed dishes, fed the baby, dressed the children, and did the marketing. In short, these were partnership marriages in the sense that both partners were interested in their respective careers and their joint family life. But not all the marriages were egalitarian. Of the only 56 husbands who were willing to help, it is apparent that they saw themselves doing just that—helping with what was essentially the wife's responsibility. For instance, one wife pointed out that her husband would do nothing on principle, "But there is nothing he has not done and will not do out of kindness." And no matter how sincere in his efforts a husband may have been he was seldom able to carry his share of the burden. The servants took their questions and complaints to the wives, and many husbands were inefficient and inadequate in their performance of domestic chores. Collier concluded that the real point was "the fact that there can be but one boss on a job at a time. Circumstances and custom usually place women in this position where the responsibility inevitably falls."[8]

A similar study, done by Cecile LaFollette in the early 1930s, did not even consider the role of the husband, either as a helper or as a true partner. The only issue were whether he approved of the wife's work and whether he was neglected because of her work. About one-fifth of the husbands in this study, or 139 out of 514 husbands, did not want their wives to work, and over half of the wives felt that they were neglecting their husbands in some way. However, 411 wives, or four-fifths of them, reported a happier companionship with their husbands. Their similar interests in work, the cooperation around the house, and their own personal growth resulted in a better understanding between these women and their husbands. Also, the extra salary made life easier for the whole family.[9]

Thus, it would seem that the working wife was in a position to develop a companionship marriage if her husband was cooperative. But the attitude of the husband was all important. By refusing to accept his wife's employment, he could destroy either her career or the marriage. In most cases, however, the attitudes of both the husband and the wife toward the latter's career made it fairly easy to adjust to the demands of family life. The wife's career was taken lightly, as a kind of hobby—a privilege that a particularly enlightened husband was willing to bestow upon his wife.[10]

There is no question that a job or career increased the responsibilities of the married woman. For most women, it meant that they were holding down two jobs. Even if they had help from servants, husbands, or children, in the last resort it was the wife who was responsible for the household.[11] [Although the added responsibility may have improved the wife's bargaining position within the family, it could not result in an egalitarian relationship as long as the husband retained his superior earning power.]

But this condition was subject to change. The man who lost his job lost status in the eyes of his family, and he often had to give way to a competent wife who was able to manage the economics of family living under adverse conditions. If she was able to make a direct contribution through earnings, she was in an even stronger position.[12] But it is doubtful that either partner accepted their new roles with enthusiasm. In writing about modern marriages in 1960, Robert Blood claimed that the dominant wife, far from being exultant over her victory, exercised power regretfully by default of her inadequate husband. He concluded: "It may be appropriate for the wife who is the sole support of her family to make most of the decisions, but it is certainly not normal for the marital roles to be reversed in this way."[13]

The fact that the husband was considered inadequate in a wife-dominant family must have made it even more difficult for the family to adjust to new roles. Men seldom accepted their lower status cheerfully. A common reaction in the 1920s, as it is today, was to withdraw from the family, either emotionally or physically, thereby inviting further contempt and disrespect, while increasing the responsibility and authority of the wife. This situation, if accompanied by desertion, divorce, or juvenile delinquency, as was often said to be the case, was referred to by sociologists as "family disorganization."[14]

The wife-dominated family was not necessarily disorganized in itself. Indeed, a woman strong enough to defy cultural tradition and her own inclination was often able to provide a strong organizing force to an unstable family. But her family was probably still susceptible to disorganization, because one family member was trying to fulfill two roles, and usually under adverse social and economic conditions. The situation was common even in the years before 1929, and the economic crisis of the 1930s exacerbated the conditions that led to family disorganization.

The changing pattern of family relations under the impact of the Depression was the subject of several studies during those years. Samual A. Stouffer and Paul E. Lazarsfeld, in their work for the Social Science Research Council, advanced the hypothesis that women probably increased their authority within the family because they fared better than men with respect to employment, at least in the early years of the Depression. Thus, some married women may have increased their contributions to the support of the family at the same time that their husbands were experiencing unemployment or a decline in earnings.[15]

This hypothesis is based upon two assumptions: that wives found employment more easily than husbands, and that the employment of the wife strengthened her position within the family. Although it was difficult to show the direct relationship between the husband's unemployment and the wife's employment on any large scale, the second assumption was probably true to some extent. A working wife improved her status within the family, but she seldom became the dominant partner, unless the husband defaulted on his responsibilities. Family studies done during the Depression present no cases in which the husband took over the household and child care responsibilities, although some men offered greater or lesser degrees of help to their working wives.

Although the unemployment of the husband did not always result in the employment of the wife, it usually brought about a change in family relationships. The causes of the change were often complex and were not necessarily economic alone. Mirra Komarovsky found that the unemployed husband lost status in 13 out of 58 families studied in the 1930s.

The decline was usually related to the fact of unemployment, but deterioration in the man's personality and his continual presence in the home also contributed to his loss of status.[16]

Komarovsky also observed the effects of different family authority patterns upon the husband's status during unemployment. When the husband's authority was primary rather than instrumental—that is, when it was based upon love and respect rather than upon his provider role—the family showed a remarkable stability in the face of unemployment. Out of the 35 cases in which the husband exercised primary authority, only two showed a deterioration in his status. But in the 12 families in which the husband possessed instrumental authority, in eight cases he experienced a decline in power. Of the 11 families with mixed attitudes, the father declined in power in three cases.[17]

In the patriarchal family, subordination to the unemployed husband might continue through habit, but if the role of provider was important to the patriarchal structure, the loss of that role could disrupt the whole concept of the husband's prerogatives. A man involved in a companionship marriage was likely to fare better than one who gained his status through tradition or his job: "For the wife who admired and loved her husband for personal qualities and was not brought up in strongly patriarchal traditions, his role of provider may be less intimately tied up with the whole complex of her attitudes."[18]

Komarovsky also suggested that in some cases the matriarchal family may have experienced greater stability than the male-dominated family when faced with an economic crisis. In the matriarchal family, the whole marital relationship was likely to be characterized by the husband's dependence upon the wife, so that unemployment did not result in a sudden change in relations. For the wife who had no illusions about her husband but who loved him in a protective and maternal way, his failure to secure a job may have come as no surprise.[19]

Thus, the unemployed man's status in the family depended upon factors beyond the loss of his provider role. His own adaptation to his loss was important, including his attitude toward the family, his willingness to help them in various ways, and the maintenance of his morale. But his wife's attitude toward him, both before and during his unemployment, was also an important factor. If the father was to maintain his position with his children, he had to maintain it with his wife: "Apparently the father does not rule alone. His prestige needs the mother's endorsement."[20]

Komarovsky's observation points to a shift in the basis of marital authority, which was becoming increasingly obvious during the twentieth century. John French and Bertram Raven distinguished five types of social power: coercive, reward, expert, legitimate, and referent. By "referent," they meant power that is referred to the husband out of respect and affection. As for the first four categories, the husband's hold on a position of authority has weakened in varying degrees in the twentieth century, but referent power continues to ensure the existence of the traditional family. As long as the husband can gain this respect from his wife, his position is secure, and most women are reluctant to withhold it.[21] During the Depression, an unemployed man may have lost power based on the first four categories, but unless he failed to function as a family member, he could still hope for referent authority, especially if he was the head of a family with strong primary attitudes rather than instrumental ones.

This point was supported in a study done by Ruth Cavan and Katherine H. Ranck in the late 1930s. They reported that well-organized families, even when greatly affected by the Depression, continued to be well-organized, whereas initially disorganized families became further disorganized. Adjustment to the crisis was as much or more an attribute of family organization as of the degree of external pressure exerted by the Depression. Cavan's and Ranck's definition of a "well-organized" family was not inconsistent with the standards of the modern companionship marriage. The criteria included unity in family objectives and ideals, the subordination of personal ambitions to family goals, satisfaction of personal interests within the family group, and an acceptance of definitely assigned and complementary roles. But most of the families they studied who met this description, or 39 out of 49 families, fell into a traditional authority pattern with the father dominant economically, the mother dominant in household matters, and a sharing in the control of the children. Cavan did not specify the actual degree of authority in each of these spheres; she only described an ideal model, which when put into practice may have varied considerably. Only nine families in the well-organized group had parents who reversed their roles in the Depression, with the mother becoming the dominant partner. In seven of these cases the mother was now the major wage-earner and had also assumed dominance in other ways. However, in other families where the mother worked the father retained his dominance. Thus, the employment of the mother could result in increased authority for her, but it was not necessarily the key to her dominance.[22] In short, Cavan and Ranck saw the adjustment of the family to the Depression as a function of the adjustment of family members to each other.

Likewise, Robert C. Angell argued that the vulnerability of the family to the Depression varied inversely with the family's integration and adaptation. By "integration," he meant a family unity based upon kindly feelings, common activities, mutuality of interests, and family ambition and pride. The pride had to derive from the qualities of the family members themselves and from the community recognition they had received, rather than from material possessions. But Angell stressed flexibility as much as family integration in adjusting to Depression conditions. Thus, if the wife became the chief breadwinner, an adaptable family would be able to rationalize the change through new concepts of member roles. Similarly, the adaptable family would be able to accept a lower standard of living in the face of necessity without losing its coherence. Conditions that produced rigidity rather than flexibility in family structure included a materialistic philosophy of life which made family members attach great importance to their standard of living, traditionalism in family mores, and irresponsibility of one or both parents.[23]

Materialistic values were most likely to occur in modern middle-class families who had responded enthusiastically to the consumerism of the 1920s. But these families were also apt to be flexible with respect to roles. In contrast, rural families, recent migrants to urban areas, and ethnic families were probably less materialistic but were more likely to hold traditional values that made it difficult for them to adapt to new family roles. Irresponsibility on the part of parents was most likely to occur either in lower-class families, where inadequacies had already become apparent aside from the effects of economic crisis, or in middle-class families in which one or both parents were unable to readjust their values under the pressure of the Depression.

Of these three types of families—middle-class, traditional, and lower-class—the first was likely to prove the most adaptable under pressure, and the most willing and energetic in accepting new values and new roles. But much depended upon the level of family integration. Angell, Cavan, and Komarovsky all stress the fact that families who were able to meet the crisis of the Depression successfully possessed qualities of strength before the Depression occurred. Those who became disorganized had weaknesses in their family structure which were merely evoked by the Depression rather than caused by it.

Thus, the Depression itself had little disorganizing effect upon successful families, even though it may have caused a considerable decline in their standard of living and a readjustment to new member roles. The wife in such a family probably already had a voice in family matters, although in most cases she recognized her husband as head of the household. If she was forced to work owing to her husband's unemployment, her position might be strengthened somewhat, but basically her work was recognized as a temporary expedient, and the traditional authority pattern was sustained.

But many families had weaknesses before the Depression, with respect to either their material values, their inflexibility in the face of changing roles, or their internal structure. Often it was individual family members who created the problem, rather than the family as a unit. There is general agreement among students of the Depression family that men tended to be less flexible than women in meeting the crisis. Angell suggested that the loss of economic security weighed most heavily upon the man, whereas the woman had her household routine to distract and sustain her. Cavan noted that men felt more keenly the personal loss of status as well as the loss of accustomed activity. Komarovsky felt that the man's loss was threefold: he lost his provider role, his prestige, and his daily work routine. Although men varied in their reaction to these losses, there is no doubt that most of them had a difficult time adjusting, and many of them stubbornly resisted role change or a new concept of family patterns.[24]

A man in this situation was particularly vulnerable if he insisted upon maintaining a rigid patriarchal system or if his position rested upon instrumental values rather than primary ones. If his economic loss was severe, a major shift in power could result in his withdrawal or desertion. C. Wight Bakke reported on a number of case histories that illustrate the impact of the Depression upon families with internal weaknesses, which were usually related to the insecure or false position of the husband. Often the parents of these families were foreign-born or of foreign-parentage, and frequently the husband was overly dominant and simply unable to sustain his authority in the face of economic inadequacies. Bakke described a generalized pattern of family adjustment through several stages of economic decline. The first stage was the initial unemployment of the man. The second stage, which he called "unstable equilibrium," was particularly critical for the man's prestige. Often the woman attempted gainful employment during this stage, and although the division of domestic chores remained the same in the sense that the wife was still responsible for the household, she assumed a greater degree of responsibility for the management and distribution of the available income. Meanwhile, the husband became discouraged by his unsuccessful search for work, and he was likely to withdraw from parental responsibilities, leaving to his wife most of the decisions regarding the activities of the children.[25]

During the third stage, which Bakke called "disorganization," the wife definitely took over the responsibility for managing and planning, although the customary division of labor with respect to domestic chores was maintained. The husband might retain his nominal position as head of the house, but both he and the other family members recognized it as titular only. Even the mother's authority was not necessarily unchallenged. If there were older children who were earning money, she might find it difficult to establish her own prestige on a level sufficient to enable her to fulfill her responsibilities. No one in the family had a clear-cut status which was recognized and customary, and the resultant conflict was often a serious handicap to family harmony. According to Bakke, if the disorganization continued for any length of time, the family could be destroyed as a unit.[26]

Thus, although the woman often bore the entire burden of family responsibilities during the Depression, she was seldom openly acknowledged to be head of the household, except in extreme cases where the husband deserted the family and the children were too small to challenge their mother's authority. These instances happened often, too, but a woman in such a situation rarely considered it a personal victory or in any way advantageous to herself or her family.

When the husband remained with the family, and when there were older children present, the woman found it difficult to establish her authority in any clear-cut fashion because the economic system and societal pressure worked against her potential leadership. Even as a gainful worker, she had a low economic status in the community. Her economic contribution to the family was bound to be lower than that previously earned by her husband, and it was probably lower than her sons' earnings. But more important, custom and tradition made it almost impossible for most families to accept a radical change in family structure while the husband was present. Most wives were themselves reluctant to usurp their husband's authority and to assert their own.

Thus, although the Depression often resulted in increased responsibilities for women, the responsibilities were always a burden and rarely redefined roles in a way that would permit women much self-assertion. Instead of being free to participate in activities beyond the family, women faced the double task of maintaining it both economically and emotionally. If the father deserted or dropped out of family activities, a matriarchal family could be said to exist, but it faced all the handicaps, both social and economic, that are the lot of a woman-dominant organization in America. It is thus no wonder that few women exulted in this enforced leadership; it was undertaken at great cost to themselves and their families.

Attitudes toward the long-term arrangements of power within the marriage relationship changed little as a result of the Depression. But there was a change in attitudes toward working wives and mothers. It was probably experienced by the children of the Depression rather than by the adult generation, and it had its greatest impact upon families of the 1950s and 1960s. E. E. LeMaster, in a study of life-styles among blue-collar workers in the early 1970s, pointed out that although his subjects overwhelmingly favored traditional male-dominant roles, over 90 percent of them were willing to have their wives work outside of the home. For some of the older men, this attitude dated back to the Depression; for others, World War II was the formative event. These men had evolved "a female model that is extremely functional for them: it allows them great freedom; guarantees them good care of their homes and their children; assures them of sexual satisfaction; protects them against ridicule and gossip; and at the same time gives them economic aid when they need it." As one of LeMaster's female interviewees responded, "Why the hell wouldn't they like a wife like that? It's a damn good deal for them!"[27] For these men, a working wife did not necessarily change her family status. Work was an added responsibility which might or might not result in more prestige or privilege. Whether it did usually depended upon the personal resources of the individual marriage partners rather than upon their economic contributions.

A number of theories of conjugal power have been advanced. For instance, greater involvement or interest in a particular issue results in greater power for the involved person. Thus, the housewife has more influence than the husabnd in strictly household matters. The same principle can be applied to community affairs and social activities. The partner showing the most interest, either through work or through children-related activities, tends to exert the most influence in either of these areas.[28]

But in times of conflict, other factors come into play, such as the relative importance of each spouse to the well-being of the other. This importance is based on their respective resources, such as their relative earning power, educational level, and competence as a homemaker, parent, sex partner, or companion. A modification of the "interest theory" was advanced by David Heer, who suggested that the power of each spouse is determined by his or her estimate of the contribution of the other as measured against his or her own opportunities outside of the marriage: "The greater the difference between the value to the wife of the resources contributed by her husband and the value to the wife of the resources which she might earn outside the existing marriage, the greater the power of her husband, and vice versa."[29]

Peter Blau offered a broader interpretation, which he called the "exchange value theory." Basically, the more alternatives that a woman has outside of her marriage, in terms of work or remarriage, the stronger her position within the marriage. Thus, a husband who is an unsuccessful provider is at a disadvantage because his wife may be able to do as well for herself without him. Similarly, a woman who is sexually attractive is in a strong position because she may have other marriage alternatives. This theory makes it possible to explain many of the variations in power in marital relationships. For instance, mothers of preschool children have less power in the family than they did before the children were born, even though their contribution to the well-being of the family has increased and, in fact, is essential. But their alternatives outside of the family are greatly restricted, and they are dependent upon their husbands for economic and emotional support.[30]

When these theories of conjugal power are considered in light of the social trends of the twentieth century, it would appear that women's status within the marital relationship was strengthened considerably. By the 1920s, two major factors, the participation of women in the work force and the declining birth rate, had operated to increase their alternatives to marriage or within marriage and to lessen their dependence upon their spouses. The Depression probably intensified these advantages, as men's economic opportunities diminished and women increased their relative contribution to family support.

However, it would not do to overemphasize the gains made by women. The values of the 1920s and 1930s stressed the joys of family life and sexual fulfillment, making it almost imperative for women to attain these goals, in spite of other possible alternatives. And whereas some demographic trends strengthened women's position, others had an opposite effect. For instance, even as marriage was viewed as the only source of happiness for women, the marriage market was becoming more competitive. The favorable male-female sex ratio of the nineteenth century was no longer operative, and women had more difficulty finding marriage partners than did men. During the Depression the problem became particularly acute as more and more men were forced to postpone marriage.[31]

Nonetheless, most of the social trends affecting family life were favorable to women. The gradual emergence of the companionship marriage among middle-class families certainly reflected a new understanding of family power relations, even if the basic husband-dominant structure remained the norm. The values of the companionship marriage, while not strictly egalitarian, created an environment more conducive to equality than the traditional family form based on patriarchal principles. It is difficult to know how widely these values were accepted, for sex segregation in work roles and leisure activities is still accepted by large segments of the population.[32] But the more successful families of the 1930s were apparently adapting to the Depression by accepting flexible member roles and new values.

It has been suggested that the Depression may have had a beneficial effect upon the long-term trend toward companionship marriage. The family assumed a new importance during a time of crisis, as more people found their entertainment at home, listening to the radio and sharing in the labor-intensive activities which characterized a lower standard of living.[33] But the stress of economic hardship and continual insecurity may also have had a detrimental effect upon family relations. Glen Elder, in a study of family life during the Depression, suggested that the economic crisis had a negative impact upon the trend toward companionship marriage: "These conditions often brought instrumental values to the fore and severely strained the fabric of companionship . . . the evidence suggests that social and economic security favors the emergence of companionship values and their expression in family relationships."[34]

Elder also suggested that the Depression had an impact upon women's roles that carried into the post war years and which strongly affected the familism of the 1950s. For instance, the example of working mothers influenced young people to accept the role in their own family life, as Le-Master found among skilled blue-collar workers. But, Elder argued, although women's activities changed, the behavioral development far exceeded any corresponding value change. That is, young people who grew up during the Depression viewed working wives and mothers not as the norm but as a response to unusual circumstances. In particular, Elder stressed the strong domestic orientation of girls who were the products of economically deprived households. The family strain in such a home could result in emotional estrangement from the father, centrality for the mother's role, an early involvement of the daughter in household work, and a lack of parental support for the daughter's higher education.[35]

The deprived household created a conducive environment for traditional sex roles and an accelerated movement toward adulthood. Children took on adult-like responsibilities at an early age. Girls were drawn into the household operation and were oriented toward a domestic future by this experience as well as by the constraints against their education. Thus, young women who grew up in deprived households developed family-centered values and a view of life that emphasized responsibility rather than self-fulfillment. Traditional male roles were also reinforced in deprived households, but boys were liberated from parental control as they were forced to take upon themselves economic responsibilities at an early age. Unlike their sisters, boys were oriented toward the world beyond the family: "Work roles involved boys from deprived homes in adult-like experiences beyond family boundaries, enlarged their sphere of know-how, and brought greater awareness to matters of economic independence and vocation."[36]

According to Elder, many of the features of child socialization during the Depression resulted from the child's adaptation to the economic and functional needs of the family. There was little concern with preparing children for the future. Rather, there was an emphasis upon family values and family roles at the expense of individualistic achievement. The young people raised in this environment carried into their adult lives the "familistic aura" that was to characterize the postwar years.[37]

The Depression performed perhaps the greatest disservice for young people, and for young women in particular, by causing many of them to lose that vision of their own potential which is essential to achievement beyond the ordinary routine of work and family. As Elder pointed out, the centrality of marriage and the family in their value system would have prevented them from seeing economic opportunities even if they had existed: "There upbringing was fashioned by the maintenance requirements of households beset by heavy economic loss, not by a vision of future options for women, and consequently had little to offer a generation which would soon encounter radical change in the technology of homemaking."[38]

In conclusion, for many women the overall effect of the Depression upon their position in the family was to bring both increased powers and increased responsibilities, although the responsibilities were likely to outweigh the powers. And the woman who had dominance in the family was at such a disadvantage in the broader society that her position could hardly be seen as desirable. The career feminists of those years equated emancipation with a job, but few working women clung to this illusion. To them, a job was an additional family responsibility, which may have given them more influence in the family circle, but which hardly had the effect of freeing them from the physical burdens and cultural norms of their times. Feminism, in the sense of a career or an ideological commitment, had little appeal to either the distraught wife of an uncooperative husband or the contented wife who worked together with her husband to overcome a family crisis.

Most American women have always considered marriage a full-time job, and indeed it has been full-time through most of the country's history. But in the 1920s new attitudes emerged with respect to the range of women's activities. Women were encouraged to more beyond the home by the women's movement of earlier decades, as well as by increased economic opportunities for women, technological developments affecting housework, and a new social morality. The Depression of the 1930s put a brake on these emergent trends and fostered the domestic climate in which marriage and family were regarded as a total commitment for women. This trend prevailed through the 1950s, and not until the 1960s did women again join a national trend toward greater self-orientation in terms of individual fulfillment.

Epilogue

The question which underlies this analysis of women's domestic and economic roles concerns the fate of feminism as an ideology and a movement in the two decades after the passage of the Nineteenth Amendment. But it is difficult to analyze the fate of feminism without an understanding of the importance of work and family in the lives of American women, and the relationship of these two roles to each other. The simple truth is that most American women, in opposition to the feminist ideology, regarded their family role as primary, and this view affected their attitudes toward their work and toward feminism.

Until recently historians have tended to agree that feminism declined, became irrelevant, or disappeared as women gave themselves over to the fads of the 1920s and the fears of the 1930s. A number of explanations for the decline of feminism have been offered, all of which contain a certain amount of truth. One of the most obvious might be loosely labeled the "let-down" explanation. That is, American feminists of the 1920s suffered a let-down after losing the issue of suffrage as a unifying cause. They were unable to find a rallying point that had the same broad appeal. Thus, they could no longer attract the kind of support that had been theirs in the years immediately preceding the passage of the suffrage amendment.[1]

Anne Firor Scott presented a more optimistic interpretation of this let-down among southern women, arguing that although the removal of legal barriers to women's participation in politics did not lead large numbers of women into political or civic responsibility, there was a "post-suffrage burst of political and social effort." The franchise therefore added another dimension to women's lives and an alternative to a purely domestic experience.[2]

A second explanation for the decline of feminism, closely related to the first, emphasizes the factionalism of women in the 1920s. Not only did feminists break into a number of factions, concentrating on a host of issues, but more important, the movement developed an ideological split over the Equal Rights Amendment. The social feminists placed protective legislation for women and children ahead of equal rights because they felt that women needed protection more than equality. The Woman's party, in contrast, was more concerned with women's rights than social reform and felt that the Equal Rights Amendment was a natural and necessary extension of the political rights gained under the Nineteenth Amendment. The two groups effectively undermined each other's efforts at reform, thereby contributing to the general decline of the woman's movement.[3]

A somewhat different view of factionalism was suggested by J. Stanley Lemons, who argued that the concentration and unity of the suffrage movement was abnormal. Long before the suffrage issue dominated the movement, social feminism had developed in response to state and local issues. Once the vote was an accomplished fact, the social feminists therefore simply returned to their previous multiple purposes. Thereafter, "No single issue emerged to preserve the false unity of the suffrage question . . . Success would have to be measured by hundreds and thousands of little items from 1920 onward."[4]

Whatever internal problems the women's movement may have had, there is little doubt that the post-1920 social and political climate was not sympathetic to its cause. William O'Neill described the effects of the postwar reaction, pointing out that it hurt the social feminists more immediately than the hard-core advocates of women's rights. But over the long run, both factions failed to reach out and gain new adherents to the cause. Lois Banner noted that feminism did not appeal to the young women of the 1920s, who were primarily interested in their rebellion against Victorian culture, its mores and sexual taboos. But the rebellion was limited. The generation of the 1920s was overwhelmed by the sex-role conditioning that had remained an integral part of its upbringing. June Sochen supported this view of women's behavior during the period declaring that "consumerism and Freudianism" had overtaken the minds of young women.[5]

The decline of feminism was analyzed most thoroughly by William O'Neill. He argued that the postsuffrage feminists failed to see that the woman problem was part of a larger social question involving sex roles in American society and the entire social order. Like many American reform groups, the radical feminists were basically conservative in their approach to change. They asked only for legal equality without addressing themselves to the whole range of problems facing women who tried to make a notch for themselves in a man's world. In particular, they overemphasized politics to the neglect of other areas—economic, social, and domestic—which had a greater impact on women's lives. O'Neill also criticized the social feminists, for although they were able to place women's issues in the broader social context of an industrial society, they prevented women from securing the opportunities enjoyed by men. They justified their activities on the grounds that society was an extension of the home, and in doing so, they froze the domestic status quo. That is, they supported the traditional family system, while attacking the societal evils that were undermining it. Yet their marital and familial roles were what was preventing women from achieving full equality.[6]

O'Neill was probably correct in his analysis of the failure of feminism, but he also asked a great deal of the feminists themselves. He seemed to suggest that they should have recognized that a reorganization of American society along socialist principles was a necessary prerequisite to the full equality of women. In particular, he was critical of them because they failed to see that in order to achieve a "genuine functional equality," there had to be a revolutionizing of domestic life. Earlier feminists saw this need; Elizabeth Cady Stanton and Susan B. Anthony are cases in point. But Suzanne LaFollette, whom O'Neill regarded as the most original feminist writer of the 1920s, was the only postsuffrage feminist to recognize that marriage was the principal institution enforcing women's inferiority. LaFollette was far in advance of both the radical feminists and the social feminists in her grasp of the social realities of the woman problem.[7]

This generally negative interpretation of feminism during the 1920s and 1930s, which has almost become the conventional wisdom of women's history, is undergoing a mild revision. It has been suggested that the careerism of the 1920s was a form of feminism, albeit an individualistic one; that the women of those years were not disillusioned with their political rights and economic opportunities; and that most women's groups, though they may have split over the Equal Rights Amendment, were able to unite on other issues, such as world peace and, in particular, economic discrimination against women during the Depression. In fact, the radical feminists of the 1930s, in an effort to defend the married woman worker, ended up with the social feminist argument—that women workers were motivated by economic necessity rather than by career aspirations or desire for self-fulfillment. In other words, expediency rather than the natural right to work became the basis for the feminist position during those years.[8]

Nonetheless, in spite of considerable activity on the part of several women's groups on behalf of feminism in its several different forms, the feminists of the 1920s and 1930s failed to provide the ideological and organizational leadership necessary to inspire potential followers. They never really came to grips with the social and domestic sources of women's status in society. Unfortunately, even if they had possessed the necessary insight into the problem, it is doubtful that they could have galvanized into action the American women of those decades, for the majority were totally committed to the values of a traditional family life. Although this commitment was perhaps shaken during the 1960s and 1970s, during the two decades preceding World War II it was seldom even questioned, not only because the feminists failed to pose the question, but because most women would not have had an answer other than the one they expressed through their everyday domestic and economic activities. As O'Neill stated, the narrow legal and "careerist" perspective of the feminists made their position seem irrelevant to most women. But an attack on the family as a source of women's inferiority would hardly have solved the problem.

The real issue of women's history is not the question of what happened to feminism during any given historical period but rather of what the role of family is in women's lives and how it affects their attitudes toward work and other activities beyond the home, toward feminism, and toward their own identities. During the 1920s and 1930s, many things were happening in the realm of politics and public policy. Women faced a variety of choices and options, in spite of the oppressive social and economic climate, and they reacted to these choices in a variety of ways. There were feminists, careerists, and reformers during those years, just as there were earlier in the nineteenth century and later in the 1960s and 1970s. Although they differed in their emphasis, all stressed an active role for women. But the rhetoric of activism must be viewed in the larger context of reality, for the majority of American women placed family first. From the feminist perspective, this may have been unfortunate, but the feminist historian must seek to understand the actuality of women's experience.

Twentieth-century feminists from Charlotte Perkins Gilman to Juliet Mitchell have defined the family as the final oppressor of women.[9] Yet they have failed to see that the family was as often a source of power to women as a tool of oppression. The married woman often felt herself in a far better social and economic position than her unmarried sister. But women's status in the family was as subject to change as was their status in society as a whole, though the change may have been more gradual. Women's tendency to place family first, ahead of career and job, may even have made their adaptation to industrialization smoother than that of men, for it minimized the psychological risk-taking that has been so often thrust upon men.[10]

Since historically the great majority of women have remained committed to family life, it is a mistake to consider women's status only in relation to their position in the job market. Internal changes in family life are just as important to women's over-all status, although they are more difficult to discern. During the 1930s, as women's domestic and economic roles increased because of the Depression, many married women moved into the labor market. But most chose not to do so. Their reasons were individual and personal to some extent, but general conditions must have influenced them as much, if not more. The reality of work opportunities discouraged many women; the heavy responsibilities of family life, including housework, child care, and high expectations in both of these areas, were deterrents to others. Societal attitudes, as well as society's failure to facilitate women's entry into the job market, were still other factors. Finally, the emergence of the companionship marriage as the middle-class ideal may have caused many women to have a positive perception of their marital status. Most married women looked to the family for their psychological satisfaction and simply did not see work as a means of improving their personal status.

Feminism, as a movement and an ideology, suffered a major setback during the interwar years because it refused to recognize the continued importance of family life and family values to most American women. In the 1920s women defined their economic activities both inside and outside of the home in terms of family needs. During the 1930s these needs intensified, and feminists were unable to convince the great mass of women that there was a relationship between feminism and the well-being of families. The issue of women and the family remains a critical one for the modern feminist movement. Perhaps it is necessary for family life to be revolutionized if women are to gain full equality. But women's historical commitment to the family indicates that the revolution will have to be gentle if it is to have a broad base of support. This is truly a feminist dilemma, and one that is not much closer to being resolved today than it was half a century ago.

Appendixes

Bibliography

Notes

Index

Cost of Living

APPENDIX A

The *Monthly Labor Review* provides the best running account of the changes in the cost of living in terms of particular commodities on a monthly basis during the 1930s. The index of consumer prices for the years 1920-1970 (base = 100) gives a general sense of the cost of living in the 1930s in comparison to the decades that came before and afterward:

Year	Index	Year	Index
1920	240	1936	166
1925	210	1937	172
1929	205	1938	169
1930	200	1939	166
1931	182	1940	168
1932	163	1945	215
1933	155	1950	288
1934	160	1960	354
1935	164	1970	464[1]

Consumer Credit and Family Economics

Consumer credit was an important means of maintaining family standards of living in the 1920s and 1930s. By the end of 1922 the principal techniques of consumer credit had been developed, after a long period of gradual growth that had started during the Civil War, and thereafter consumer credit experienced a few years of enormous expansion. The outstanding amount of consumer credit doubled between the beginning of 1923 and the fall of 1924. All types of consumer credit agencies participated in this expansion, but the most rapid growth occurred among the newer specialized agencies, which used installment payment techniques, and among the older agencies whose receivables arose as by-products of installment sales.[1]

The expansion of consumer credit came to an end soon after the stock market collapse in September 1929. The sale of automobiles dropped promptly, and sales of furniture, radios, most types of household appliances, and many other durable consumer goods soon followed course. The retail automobile paper held by installment finance companies fell by 25 percent between September 1929 and September 1930. The total amount of consumer credit declined by 7 percent in 1930, 15 percent in 1931, and 23 percent in 1932.[2]

By the spring of 1933, some types of consumer credit suddenly reversed their downward trend. Automobile financing led the expansion of consumer credit, as it had led its liquidation, but other types of durable consumer goods also contributed, especially the refrigerator, which had continued to expand even in the years 1929-1933, because by 1929 the market for the product had been barely scratched. For consumer credit as a whole, there was an expansion of 9 percent in 1934, 16 percent in 1935, 22 percent in 1936, and 12 percent in 1937. The rate of expansion during the first four months of 1937 was greater than for any similar period between 1923 and 1937, and it probably exceeded that for any similar period in the history of consumer credit.[3]

The pattern of consumer credit liquidation and expansion between 1929 and 1939 shows that credit buying dropped dramatically in the early years of the Depression, but it expanded just as dramatically when the American people sensed a potential recovery (Table B.1). Much of this expansion was made possible by liberalized terms, reduced down payments, and longer periods of repayment, especially in the area of car financing.

A more detailed study of consumer financing, based upon the Consumer Purchases Study of 1935-1936, estimates consumer debt by income level. Over one-third of all nonrelief families in 1935-1936 had a net change in consumer debt in the form of installment debt, cash loan debt, or charge account purchases. The frequency of debt rose from about 28 percent in the income levels below $750 to a peak of almost 42 percent for families with incomes of 1,750-$2,000, and then declined consistently as incomes advanced until it stood at less than 23 percent for families with incomes of $5,000 or more.[4]

Table B.1. Consumer installment credit and total consumer credit outstanding at end of year, 1929-1937 (estimated)

Year	Consumer installment credit		Total consumer credit	
	Outstanding (millions of $)	Index	Outstanding (millions of $)	Index
1929	3,231	100	8,183	100
1930	2,761	85	7,570	93
1931	2,253	70	6,442	79
1932	1,533	47	4,957	61
1933	1,629	50	4,807	59
1934	1,873	58	5,222	64
1935	2,586	80	6,080	74
1936	3,452	107	7,435	91
1937	3,847	119	8,326	102

Source: Duncan McC. Holthausen, with Malcolm L. Merriam and Rolf Nugent, *The Volume of Consumer Installment Credit, 1929-38*, Financial Research Program: Studies in Consumer Installment Financing, vol. VII (New York: National Bureau of Economic Research, 1940), p. 131.

Deficit Spending

The extent to which the American people were living beyond their means in the 1930s varied according to the year and the income class. The years 1931-1934 saw a deficit in both national and personal savings, as compared to the other years in the decade (Table C.1). The pattern of saving from 1929 to 1939 is based on the social accounting concept. This measurement of savings, based upon methods of modern business accounting, is complete in the sense that it covers every aspect of the activities of an economic unit which is considered economically relevant.[1]

The American people as a whole showed personal deficits through the most severe years of the Depression, but by 1935 they showed positive savings. However, this was not true for the majority of Americans when their savings and expenditures are considered by income class (Table C.2). Most families were unable to save until they reached the income level of $1,500. Since 64.6 percent of all American families had incomes under $1,500, it is apparent that most families were living beyond their means to at least a degree.

These figures support the argument that many families maintained their customary level of expenditures through temporary periods of income reverses. Thus, the deficits of the lower income brackets can be traced to the expenditures of families who usually had higher incomes. These families did not adjust their consumption to a lower income, probably because they did not consider the shift in their income position to be a permanent one.[2]

Table C.1. National, personal, and corporate savings, 1929-1939 (millions of $)

Year	National savings	Personal savings	Corporate savings
1929	15,968	11,485	2,136
1930	5,820	5,617	−514
1931	−3,305	2,466	−3,360
1932	−10,491	−3,273	−5,032
1933	−8,851	−3,805	−4,687
1934	−4,417	−954	−2,718
1935	237	2,349	−1,287
1936	1,560	5,275	−1,405
1937	7,286	7,322	−553
1938	2,002	3,715	−574
1939	4,842	6,852	−89

Source: Raymond W. Goldsmith, *et al. A Study of Savings in the United States,* Vol. I, *Introduction: Tables of Annual Estimates of Savings, 1897 to 1949* (Princeton: Princeton University Press, 1955), p. 345.

Table C.2. Expenditures and savings of nonfarm families by income class, 1935-1936

Income class ($)	Average family size	Average income ($)	Average expenditures ($)	Average savings ($)
Under 500	3.2	292	493	−201
500-1,000	3.5	730	802	−72
1,000-1,500	3.6	1,176	1,196	−20
1,500-2,000	3.7	1,636	1,598	38
2,000-3,000	3.8	2,292	2,124	168
3,000-4,000	4.0	3,243	2,814	429
4,000-5,000	4.2	4,207	3,467	740
5,000-10,000	4.1	6,598	4,950	1,648
Over 10,000	3.8	22,259	12,109	10,150

Source: Raymond W. Goldsmith *et al., A Study of Savings in the United States,* vol. III, *Special Studies* (Princeton: Princeton University Press, 1956), pp. 182-183.

The Census of 1910

APPENDIX D

There is reason to suspect the 1910 census figures. According to Alba M. Edwards, who compiled the occupational statistics for the Bureau of the Census, the 1910 census was an anomaly because of an over enumeration of farm workers. Census enumerators were instructed not to overlook women workers and to report them as gainfully occupied even if they were unpaid family workers. Consequently, not only did the percentage of all working women go up, but the percentage of those engaged in agriculture went up from 3.3 percent to 5.2 percent of all women ten years of age and over. Since the proportion of all women living in rural areas declined during these years, such an increase seems unlikely unless it can be attributed to the method of enumeration.[1]

Edwards' solution to the problem of overenumeration was to adjust the 1910 census figures downward so as to bring them into line with the 1900 and 1920 censuses. He argued that there was no real decline in the proportion of women workers between 1910 and 1920 but merely an illusion of decline because of the overenumeration in 1910.

Later students of the labor force have had a different perspective on the value of the 1910 census. Robert Smuts, for instance, made a case for a net decrease in female labor participation from 1910 to 1930. He argued that the pre-1940 increases were apparent, not real, because over the years improved techniques, broader definitions of labor force status, and the redistribution of the female working population into categories easier to enumerate improved the accuracy of the count. Smuts suggested, therefore, that if it were possible to adjust the data, it would probably show very little increase in the labor force participation of women between 1890 and 1950. But labor force participation increased substantially after 1940, so if there was indeed little net change between 1890 and 1950, there must have been a net decrease before 1950. This is what the unadjusted census figures show for the period from 1910 to 1930, according to Smuts.[2]

Both Smuts and A. J. Jaffee maintained that the census of 1910 was a superior enumeration because it was the only one prior to 1940 that made a special effort to enumerate women workers. According to Jaffee, the procedures used in 1910 most nearly approximated the procedures now used for obtaining labor force information. That census was the first attempt to include almost everyone who could conceivably be classified as being in the work force, and hence it was the earliest census to provide data almost comparable in coverage with the labor force data for 1940 and subsequent years.[3]

The problem with this argument is that while it upholds the high proportion of women workers in 1910, it also casts suspicion upon the lower rates of 1920 and 1930. That is, there may have been more women working in those years than were enumerated. Given the problem of changing census definitions of occupations and of the term "gainful employment," the issue may never be resolved, but it points to the difficulty of using census data to show consistent trends over a period of time.

Method of Determining Occupational Classification

APPENDIX E

The several categories of workers in each year are arbitrarily designated as either white-collar, domestic and personal service, or laborers and semiskilled operatives. For instance, in 1940 professional or semiprofessional workers, clerical, sales, or kindred workers, and proprietors, managers, or officials could all be classified as white-collar. There may be exceptions within these groups, but they are not numerically significant. Craftsmen, foremen, or kindred workers, operatives or kindred workers, and laborers, including farm laborers, constitute another group—the laborers and semiskilled operatives. Service workers, except protective, parallel the domestic and personal service group.

For the 1930, 1920, and 1910 categories there are two important fields that together make up most of the laborers and semiskilled operatives. These are agriculture and manufacturing or mechanical industries. Domestic service is self-evident, and three fields—professional service, clerical occupations, and trade—constitute the white-collar occupations. The one category that is somewhat difficult to place is transportation and communication. Ordinarily, for male workers, this would probably be classified as manual labor, but 76.5 percent of the female labor force in this field in 1910, and 80 percent in 1920 and 1930, were telephone operators.[1] Since telephone operators were classified as clerical workers in 1940, for the sake of consistency, they should be classified as white-collar workers in the earlier years. Telephone operators constituted about 2.1 percent of the female work force in those years, or 80 percent of 2.6 percent. In 1910 they were 1.06 percent of the female labor force, or 76 percent of 1.4 percent.

Bibliography

In addition to the relevant government publications, including the U.S. Census Bureau reports for 1910-1940, the studies of the Department of Labor, Women's Bureau, and of the Department of Labor, Bureau of Labor Statistics, the following studies were useful to my work.

Background

Aaron, Daniel, and Bendiner, Robert, eds., *The Strenuous Decade: A Social and Intellectual Record of the Nineteen-Thirties* (New York: Anchor Books, 1970).

Bernstein, Irving, *The Lean Years: A History of the American Worker, 1920-1933* (Boston: Houghton Mifflin, 1966).

Chambers, Clarke A., *Seedtime of Reform: American Social Service and Social Action, 1918-1933* (Minneapolis: University of Minnesota Press, 1963).

Frisch, Morton J., and Diamond, Martin, eds., *The Thirties: A Reconsideration in the Light of the American Political Tradition* (DeKalb: Northern Illinois University Press, 1968).

Hession, Charles H., and Sardy, Hyman, *Ascent to Affluence: A History of American Economic Development* (Boston: Allyn and Bacon, 1969).

Hicks, John D., *Republican Ascendancy, 1921-1933* (New York: Harper, 1960).

Leuchtenburg, William E., *Franklin Roosevelt and the New Deal, 1932-1940* (New York: Harper & Row, 1964).

―――― *The Perils of Prosperity, 1914-1932* (Chicago: University of Chicago Press, 1958).

Lubove, Roy, *The Struggle for Social Security, 1900-1935* (Cambridge, Mass.: Harvard University Press, 1968).

Lynd, Robert S., and Lynd, Helen Merrell, *Middletown: A Study in Modern American Culture* (New York: Harcourt, Brace, & World, 1929).

―――― *Middletown in Transition: A Study in Cultural Conflicts* (New York: Harcourt, Brace, & World, 1937).

Ostrander, Gilman M., *American Civilization in the First Machine Age, 1890-1940* (New York: Harper & Row, 1970).

Schlesinger, Arthur M. Jr., *The Age of Roosevelt: The Crisis of the Old Order, 1919-1933* (Boston: Houghton Mifflin, 1957).

Soule, George, *Prosperity Decade, 1917-1932* (New York: Rinehart, 1947).

Trattner, Walter I., *From Poor Law to Welfare State: A History of Social Welfare in America* (New York: Macmillan, 1974).

Women

Banner, Lois W., *Women in Modern America: A Brief History* (New York: Harcourt, Brace, Jovanovich, 1974).

Breckinridge, Sophonisba P., "The Activities of Women Outside the Home," President's Research Committee on Social Trends, *Recent Social Trends* (New York: McGraw-Hill, 1933), I, 709-750.

———— *Women in the Twentieth Century: A Study of Their Political, Social and Economic Activities* (New York: McGraw-Hill, 1933).

Chafe, William H., *The American Woman: Her Changing Social, Economic, and Political Role, 1920-1970* (New York: Oxford University Press, 1972).

Freedman, Estelle B., "The New Woman: Changing Views of Women in the 1920s," *Journal of American History*, 61 (September 1974): 372-393.

Lemons, J. Stanley, *The Woman Citizen: Social Feminism in the 1920s* (Chicago: University of Illinois Press, 1973).

O'Neill, William L., *Everyone Was Brave: The Rise and Fall of Feminism in America* (Chicago: Quadrangle Books, 1969).

Scott, Ann Firor, *The Southern Lady: From Pedestal to Politics, 1830-1930* (Chicago: University of Chicago Press, 1970).

Sochen, June, *Movers and Shakers: American Women Thinkers and Activists, 1900-1970* (Chicago: Quadrangle Books, 1973).

Yellis, Kenneth, "Prosperity's Child: Some Thoughts on the Flapper," *American Quarterly*, 21 (Spring 1969): 44-64.

Labor Trends

Anderson, H. Dewey, and Davidson, Percy E., *Occupational Trends in the United States* (Stanford: Stanford University Press, 1940).

Baker, Elizabeth Faulkner, *Technology and Woman's Work* (New York: Columbia University Press, 1964).

Bancroft, Gertrude, *The American Labor Force: Its Growth and Changing Composition*, Census Monograph Series, Social Science Research Council (New York: John Wiley & Sons, 1958).

Davis, Margery, "Woman's Place is at the Typewriter: The Feminization of the Clerical Labor Force," *Radical America* 8 (July-August 1974): 1-28.

Durand, John D., *The Labor Force in the United States, 1890-1960* (New York: Social Science Research Council, 1948).

Edwards, Alba M., *Comparative Statistics for the United States, 1870-1940*, Bureau of the Census (Washington, D.C.: Government Printing Office, 1943).

———— *A Social-Economic Grouping of the Gainful Workers of the United States*, Bureau of the Census (Washington, D.C.: Government Printing Office, 1938).

Haber, Sheldon, "Trends in Work Rates of White Females, 1890-1950," *Industrial and Labor Relations Review* 26 (July 1973): 1122-1134.

Hooks, Janet M., *Women's Occupations Through Seven Decades*, Women's Bureau, Bulletin no. 218 (Washington, D.C.: Government Printing Office, 1947).

Jaffe, A. J., "Trends in the Participation of Women in the Working Force," *Monthly Labor Review* 79 (May 1956): 559-565.

Lebergott, Stanley, *Manpower in Economic Growth: The American Record since 1800* (New York: McGraw-Hill, 1964).

Long, Clarence D., *The Labor Force under Changing Income and Employment* (Princeton: Princeton University Press, 1958).

Oppenheimer, Valerie, "Demographic Influence on Female Employment and the Status of Women," in Joan Huber, ed., *Changing Women in a Changing Society* (Chicago: University of Chicago Press, 1973).

—— *The Female Labor Force in the United States: Demographic and Economic Factors Governing Its Growth and Changing Composition*, Population Monograph 5 (Berkeley: University of California Press, 1970).

Parrish, John B., "Nation's Labor Supply, 1930-1937," *American Economic Review* 29 (June 1939): 325-336.

Smuts, Robert W., "The Female Labor Force: A Case Study in the Interpretation of Historical Statistics," *Journal of the American Statistical Association* 55 (March 1960): 71-79.

Sorkin, Alan L., "On the Occupational Status of Women, 1870-1970," *American Journal of Economics and Sociology* 32 (July 1973): 235-244.

Wolfbein, Seymour, and Jaffe, A. J., "Demographic Factors in Labor Force Growth," *American Sociological Review* 11 (August 1946): 392-396.

Working Women

Anderson, Mary, *Woman at Work*, as told to Mary N. Winslow (Minneapolis: University of Minnesota Press, 1951).

Baxandall, Rosalyn, et al., *America's Working Women: A Documentary History, 1600 to the Present* (New York: Random House, 1976).

Brownlee, W. Elliot, and Brownlee, Mary M., *Women in the American Economy: A Documentary History, 1675-1929* (New Haven: Yale University Press, 1976).

Dempsey, Mary V., *The Occupational Progress of Women, 1910-1930*, Women's Bureau, Bulletin no. 104 (Washington, D.C.: Government Printing Office, 1933).

Donovan, Frances R., *The Saleslady* (Chicago: University of Chicago Press, 1929).

—— *The Woman Who Waits* (Boston: Richard G. Badger, 1920).

Elliot, Margaret, and Manson, Grace E., *Earnings of Women in Business and the Professions*, Michigan Business Studies (Ann Arbor: University of Michigan, 1930).

Hill, Joseph A., *Women in Gainful Occupations, 1870-1920, A Study of the Trend of Recent Changes in the Numbers, Occupation Distribution and*

Family Relationships of Women, Reported in the Census as Following a Gainful Occupation, Census Monographs, IX (Washington, D.C.: Government Printing Office, 1929).

Hughes, Gwendolyn Salisbury, *Mothers in Industry: Wage-Earning by Mothers in Philadelphia* (New York: New Republic, 1925).

Kelley, Florence, "Labor Legislation for Women and Its Effect on Earnings and Conditions of Labor," *Annals of the American Academy of Political and Social Sciences* 143 (May 1929): 286-300.

Kessler-Harris, Alice, "Women's Wage Work as Myth and History," *Labor History* 19 (Spring 1978): 287-301.

Klaczynska, Barbara, "Why Women Work: A Comparison of Various Groups—Philadelphia, 1910-1930," *Labor History* 17 (Winter 1976): 73-87.

Milkman, Ruth, "Women's Work and Economic Crisis: Some Lessons of the Great Depression," *Review of Radical Political Economics* 8 (Spring 1976): 73-97.

National Manpower Council, *Womanpower* (New York: Columbia University Press, 1957).

Patterson, James T., "Mary Dewson and the American Minimum Wage Movement," *Labor History* 5 (Spring 1964): 134-152.

Perkins, Frances, and Faulkner, Elizabeth, "Do Women in Industry Need Special Protection?" *Survey* 55 (Feb. 15, 1926): 529-585.

Pleck, Elizabeth W., "Two Worlds in One: Work and Family," *Journal of Social History* 9 (Winter 1976): 178-195.

Pruette, Lorine, *Women Workers Through the Depression* (New York: Macmillan, 1934).

Smuts, Robert W., *Women and Work in America* (New York: Columbia University Press, 1956).

Stricker, Frank, "Cookbooks and Law Books: The Hidden History of Career Women in Twentieth Century America," *Journal of Social History* 10 (Fall 1976): 1-19.

Whittemore, Margaret, "The Wage-Earning Homemaker and the Family Income," *Journal of Home Economics* 23 (November 1931): 998-1001.

Unemployment

Addams, Jane, "Social Consequences of Depression," *Survey* 67 (Jan. 1, 1932): 370-371.

Brandt, Lilian, *An Impressionistic View of the Winter of 1930-1931 in New York City* (New York: Welfare Council of New York City, 1932).

Clague, Ewan, and Powell, Webster, *Ten Thousand Out of Work* (Philadelphia: University of Pennsylvania Press, 1933).

Elderton, Marion, ed., *Case Studies of Unemployment* (Philadelphia: University of Pennsylvania Press, 1931).

Federal Emergency Relief Administration, *Unemployment Relief Census, October, 1933* (Washington, D.C.: Government Printing Office, 1934).

Givens, Meredith B., "Statistical Measures of Social Aspects of Unemployment," *Journal of American Statistical Association* 26 (September 1931): 303-318.

Hennion, Adelaide, "The Effects of Unemployment as Seen by a Family Society," *Smith College Studies in Social Work* 1 (1930): 66-85.

Hogg, Margaret H., *The Incidence of Work Shortage: Report of a Survey by Sample of Families Made in New Haven, Connecticut, in May-June, 1931* (New York: Russell Sage Foundation, 1932).

Jones, John Paul, "Middle-Class Misery," *Survey* 68 (Sept. 1, 1932): 402-404.

Pidgeon, Mary E., *Employment Fluctuations and Unemployment of Women: Certain Indications from Various Sources, 1928-31*, Women's Bureau, Bulletin no. 113 (Washington, D.C.: Government Printing Office, 1933).

U.S. Office of Administrator of the Census of Partial Employment, Unemployment, and Occupations, 1937, *Final Report on Total and Partial Unemployment* (Washington, D.C.: Government Printing Office, 1938), 4 vols.

Weintraub, David, and Posner, Harold L., *Unemployment and Increasing Productivity* (Philadelphia: National Research Project, 1937).

White, R. Clyde, and White, Mary K., *Research Memorandum on Social Aspects of Relief Policies in the Depression* (New York: Social Science Research Council, 1937).

Williams, J. M., *Human Aspects of Unemployment and Relief* (Chapel Hill: University of North Carolina Press, 1933).

Woytinsky, W. S., *Additional Workers and the Volume of Unemployment*, Pamphlet Series no. 1 (Washington, D.C.: Committee on Social Security of the Social Science Research Council, 1940).

Young, Pauline V., "The New Poor," *Sociology and Social Research* 17 (January-February 1933): 234-242.

————— "Human Cost of Unemployment," *Sociology and Social Research* 17 (March-April 1933): 361-369.

Zawadzki, Bohan, and Lazarsfeld, Paul, "The Psychological Consequences of Unemployment," *Journal of Social Psychology* 6 (May 1935): 224-251.

Family

Angell, Robert C., *The Family Encounters the Depression* (New York: Charles Scribner's Sons, 1936).

Anthony, Katharine, "The Family," in Harold E. Stearns, ed., *Civilization in the United States* (New York: Harcourt, Brace, 1922).

Bakke, E. Wight, *Citizens Without Work: A Study of the Effects of Unemployment upon the Workers' Social Relations and Practices* (New Haven: Yale University Press, 1940).

Byrne, Harriet A., *The Effects of the Depression on Wage Earners' Families*, Women's Bureau, Bulletin no. 108 (Washington, D.C.: Government Printing Office, 1933).

Cavan, Ruth S., and Ranck, Katherine H., *The Family and the Depression: A Study of One Hundred Chicago Families* (Chicago: University of Chicago Press, 1938).

Glick, Paul, *American Families*, Census Monograph Series (New York: John Wiley, 1957).

Goodsell, Willystine, *Problems of the Family* (New York: Century, 1928).

Groves, Ernest R., *Social Problems of the Family* (Philadelphia: J. B. Lippincott, 1927).

Komarovsky, Mirra, *The Unemployed Man and His Family: The Effect of Unemployment upon the Status of the Man in Fifty-Nine Families* (New York: Dryden Press, 1940).

Monroe, Day, *Chicago Families: A Study of Unpublished Data* (Chicago: University of Chicago Press, 1932).

Morgan, Winona L., *The Family Meets the Depression* (Minneapolis: University of Minnesota Press, 1939).

Mowrer, Ernest, *Family Disorganization: An Introduction to a Sociological Analysis* (Chicago: University of Chicago Press, 1932).

Ogburn, William F., "The Changing Family," *The Family* 19 (July 1938): 139-143.

———— "The Family and Its Functions," in President's Research Committee on Social Trends, *Recent Social Trends* (New York: McGraw-Hill, 1933), I, 661-708.

———— "Recent Changes in Marriage," *American Journal of Sociology* 41 (November 1935): 285-298.

Stouffer, Samuel A., and Lazarsfeld, Paul E., *Research Memorandum on the Family in the Depression*, Bulletin no. 29 (New York: Social Science Research Council, 1937).

Thurston, Flora M., *A Bibliography of Family Relationships* (New York: National Council of Parent Education, 1932).

Family Income and Expenditures

Douglas, Paul H., "The Changing Basis of Family Support and Expenditure," in Margaret E. Rich, ed., *Family Life Today* (New York: Houghton Mifflin, 1928).

———— *Real Wages in the United States, 1890-1926* (New York: Houghton Mifflin, 1930).

———— et al., *The Worker in the Modern Economic Society* (Chicago: University of Chicago Press, 1926).

Gross, Irma H., and Pond, Julia, *Changes in Standards of Consumption during a Depression*, Michigan Agricultural Experiment Station, Special Bulletin 274 (July 1936).

Houghteling, Lelia, *The Income and Standard of Living of Unskilled Laborers in Chicago* (Chicago: University of Chicago Press, 1927).

Kyrk, Hazel, *Economic Problems of the Family* (New York: Harper & Brothers, 1933).

———— *Theory of Consumption* (New York: Houghton Mifflin, 1923).

Lamale, Helen Humes, "Changes in Concepts of Income Adequacy over the Last Century," in Papers and Proceedings of the Seventieth Annual Meeting, *American Economic Review* 48 (May 1958): 291-299.

Leven, Maurice, et al., *America's Capacity to Consume* (Washington, D.C.: Brookings Institution, 1934).

Lynd, Robert S., "The People as Consumers," in President's Research Committee on Social Trends, *Recent Social Trends* (New York: McGraw-Hill, 1933), II, 857-911.

Nystrom, Paul H., *Economic Principles of Consumption* (New York: Ronald Press, 1929).

Vaile, Roland S., *Research Memorandum on Social Aspects of Consumption in the Depression* (New York: Social Science Research Council, 1937).

Wolman, Leo, *Consumption and the Standard of Living* (New York: McGraw-Hill, 1929), 2 vols.

Women in the Home

Andrews, Benjamin R., *Economics of the Household* (New York: Macmillan, 1923; rev. 1935).

Calverton, Victor F., and Schmalhausen, Samuel D., eds., *The New Generation: The Intimate Problems of Modern Parents and Children* (New York: Macaulay, 1930).

Groves, Ernest R., "Parent Education," *Annals of the American Academy of Political and Social Science* 160 (March 1932): 216-222.

Judy, Helen E., "Homemaking in This Modern Age," *Journal of American Association of University Women*, January 1934.

—— *Trends in Home Management*, Contributions to Education, no. 365 (New York: Bureau of Publications, Teachers College, Columbia University, 1929).

Kennedy, David M., *Birth Control in America: The Career of Margaret Sanger* (New Haven: Yale University Press, 1970).

Kiser, C. V., "Trends in Annual Birth Rates among Married Women in Selected Areas According to Nativity, Age, and Social Class," *Milbank Memorial Fund Quarterly* 15 (January 1937): 1-27.

Kneeland, Hildegarde, "Women's Economic Contribution in the Home," *Annals of the American Academy of Political and Social Sciences* 143 (May 1929): 33-40.

Kneeland, Hildegarde, "Is the Modern Housewife a Lady of Leisure?" *Survey* 62 (June 1, 1929): 301-302.

Lotka, Alfred J., and Spiegelman, Mortimer, "The Trend of the Birth Rate by Age of Mother and Order of Birth," *Journal of the American Statistical Association* 35 (December 1940): 595-601.

Richardson, Anna E., "The Woman Administrator in the Home," *Annals of the American Academy of Political and Social Science* 143 (May 1929): 21-32.

Shyrock, H. S., Jr., "Trends in Age Specific Fertility Rates," *Milbank Memorial Fund Quarterly* 17 (July 1939): 294-307.

Steere, Geoffrey H., "Freudianism and Child-Rearing in the Twenties," *American Quarterly* 20 (Winter 1968): 759-767.

Watson, Amy E., "The Reorganization of Household Work," *Annals of the American Academy of Political and Social Science* 160 (March 1932): 165-178.

Woodhouse, Chase Going, "The New Profession of Homemaking," *Survey* 57 (Dec. 1, 1926): 316-317.

Children and Youth

Bremner, Robert H., ed., *Children and Youth in America: A Documentary History*, vol. II, *1866-1932* (Cambridge, Mass.: Harvard University Press, 1971).

Buffum, Anne W., "Children of Working Women," *American Federationist* 38 (March 1931): 301-304.

Centers, Richard, "Children of the New Deal: Social Stratification and Adolescence," in Reinhard Bendix and S. M. Lipset, eds., *Class, Status, and Power* (New York: Free Press of Glencoe, 1953), pp. 359-370.

Elder, Glen H., Jr., *Children of the Great Depression: Social Change in Life Experience* (Chicago: University of Chicago Press, 1974).

Frank, Lawrence K., "Childhood and Youth," in President's Research Committee on Social Trends, *Recent Social Trends* (New York: McGraw-Hill, 1933), II, 751-800.

Kett, Joseph F., *Rites of Passage: Adolescence in America, 1790 to the Present* (New York: Basic Books, 1977).

Lenroot, Katharine F., "Child Welfare, 1930-1940," *Annals of the American Academy of Political and Social Science* 212 (November 1940): 1-11.

Lumpkin, Katharine D., and Douglas, Dorothy W., *Child Workers in America* (New York: International Publishers, 1937).

McClenahan, Bessie A., "The Child of the Relief Agency," *Social Forces* 13 (1935): 560-567.

Menefee, Louis Arnold, and Chambers, M. M., *American Youth: An Annotated Bibliography* (Washington, D.C.: American Council on Education, 1938).

Minehan, Thomas, *Boy and Girl Tramps of America* (New York: Farrar and Rinehart, 1934).

Trattner, Walter I., *Crusade for the Children: A History of the National Child Labor Committee and Child Labor Reform in America* (Chicago: Quadrangle Books, 1970).

White House Conference, *The Adolescent in the Family* (New York: Appleton-Century, 1934).

White House Conference on Child Health and Protection, *The Young Child in the Home* (New York: Appleton-Century, 1936).

Wright, Helen R., *Children of Wage-Earning Mothers*, U.S. Department of Labor, Children's Bureau, Publication no. 102 (Washington, D.C.: Government Printing Office, 1922).

Notes

Introduction

1. See e.g. Alice Kessler-Harris, "Review Essay: Women's Wage Work as Myth and History," *Labor History* 19 (Spring 1978): 287-307; Kessler-Harris, "Women, Work, and the Social Order," in Berenice A. Carroll, ed., *Liberating Women's History: Theoretical and Critical Essays* (Chicago: University of Illinois Press, 1976), pp. 330-343; Thomas Dublin, "Women, Work, and the Family: Women Operatives in the Lowell Mills, 1830-1860," *Labor History* 16 (Winter 1975): 99-116; Virginia Yans-McLaughlin, "A Flexible Tradition: South Italian Immigrants Confront a New Work Experience," *Journal of Social History* 7 (Summer 1974): 429-445; Barbara Klaczynska, "Why Women Work: A Comparison of Various Groups—Philadelphia, 1910-1930," *Labor History* 17 (Winter 1976): 73-87; in Milton Cantor and Bruce Laurie, eds., *Class, Sex, and the Woman Worker* (Westport, Conn.: Greenwood Press, 1977), see Susan J. Kleinberg, "The Systematic Study of Urban Women," pp. 20-42; Carol Groneman, "She Earns as a Child: She Pays as a Man: Women Workers in a Mid-Nineteenth Century New York City Community," pp. 83-100; Virginia Yans-McLaughlin, "Italian Women and Work: Experience and Perception," pp. 101-120; Joan W. Scott and Louise A. Tilly, "Women's Work and the Family in Nineteenth-Century Europe," *Comparative Studies in Society and History* 17 (January 1975): 36-64; Martha Norby Fraundorf, "The Labor Force Participation of Turn-of-the-Century Married Women," *Journal of Economic History* 39 (June 1979): 401-418; Leslie Woodcock Tentler, *Wage-Earning Women: Industrial Work and Family Life in the United States, 1900-1930* (New York: Oxford University Press, 1979).

2. See Leslie Houghteling, *The Income and Standard of Living of Unskilled Laborers in Chicago* (Chicago: University of Chicago Press, 1927); Katharine Anthony, "The Family," in H. E. Stearns, ed., *Civilization in the United States* (New York: Harcourt, Brace, 1922); Henry L. Lurie, "Economic Stabilization of the Family: The Standard of Living," *National Conference of Social Work* (New York: Conference Bulletin, 1928), p. 292; Karl de Schweinitz, "Are the Poor Really Poor?" *Survey* 59 (Jan. 15, 1928): 517; Abraham Epstein, "Have American Wages Permitted an American Standard of Living?" *Annals of the American Academy of Political and Social Science* 99 (September 1921): 169-190.

3. See, Winifred D. Wandersee Bolin, "Past Ideals and Present Pleasures:

Women, Work, and Family, 1920-1940," unpubl. diss., University of Minnesota, 1976, pp. 104-107.

4. As there were always women who worked for personal fulfillment, social enjoyment, or some other noneconomic reason, there is no need to justify women's wage labor activities as a product of economic need. See Kessler-Harris, "Review Essay," p. 290. Nonetheless, economic factors, however they may have been defined or perceived, had an important impact upon women's tendency to labor force participation.

5. Although some feminists view the Western family as patriarchal, male-dominated, and therefore oppressive to women, the pattern is far more complex, especially in the twentieth century. See Juliet Mitchell, *Woman's Estate* (New York: Vintage Books, 1971), p. 99; Dair L. Gillespie, "Who Has the Power? The Marital Struggle," in Hans Peter Dreitzel, ed., *Family, Marriage, and the Struggle of the Sexes* (New York: Macmillan, 1972), pp. 121-150.

6. See William L. O'Neill, *Everyone Was Brave: A History of Feminism in America* (Chicago: Quadrangle Books, 1969); William H. Chafe, *The American Woman: Her Changing Social, Economic, and Political Role, 1920-1970* (New York: Oxford University Press, 1972); Lois W. Banner, *Women in Modern America: A Brief History* (New York: Harcourt, Brace, Jovanovich, 1974); June Sochen, *Movers and Shakers: American Women Thinkers and Activists, 1900-1970* (New York: Quadrangle Books, 1973).

7. See, Winifred D. Wandersee Bolin, "The Modernization of the American Family as an Economic Unit: The Role of Women and Children," paper presented at Organization of American Historians, Annual Conference, New Orleans, April 11-14, 1979.

1. The Economics of Family Life

1. Royal Meeker, "What Is the American Standard of Living?" *Monthly Labor Review* 9 (July 1919): 1.

2. Paul H. Douglas, *Real Wages in the United States, 1890-1926* (New York: Houghton Mifflin, 1930), p. 584.

3. Ibid.

4. Anonymous, "Living on the Ragged Edge: Family Income vs. Family Expenses," *Harper's Magazine* 152 (December 1925): 54-59. See also Edward Moth Woolley, "Scraping By on a Few Thousand a Year," *Collier's* 74 (Oct. 25, 1924): 12-13; "The Family's Problem: We're Up Against It—We Young Folks Who Haven't Money Enough to Get Married," *American Magazine* 106 (November 1928): 192; "Our Double-Standard Prosperity," *Literary Digest* 101 (May 18, 1929): 83-85; "Is It Safe to Marry on $20 a Week? Omaha Says Yes," *Literary Digest* 76 (Jan. 2, 1923): 46-51.

5. See Helen E. Judy, *Trends in Home Management*, Contributions to Education, no. 365 (New York: Bureau of Publications, Teacher's College, Columbia University 1929); Benjamin R. Andrew, *Economics of the Household* (New York: Macmillan, 1923); Howard French Bigelow, *Family Finance: A Study in the Economics of Consumption* (Chicago: J. B. Lippincott, 1936). See also, Margaret

Matlack, "The Bride and the Budget," *Ladies Home Journal* 40 (September 1923): 100.

6. William F. Ogburn, "The Family and Its Functions," in *Recent Social Trends* (New York: McGraw-Hill, 1933), I, 664-666.

7. Maurice Leven, Harold G. Moulton, and Clark Warburton, *America's Capacity to Consume* (Washington, D.C.: Brookings Institution, 1934), p. 56.

8. Faith M. Williams and Helen Connolly, *Bibliography on Studies of Costs and Standards of Living in the United States*, U.S. Bureau of Home Economics (Washington, D.C.: Government Printing Office, 1930).

9. See E. L. Kirkpatrick, *The Farmer's Standard of Living* (New York: Century, 1929); Carle E. Zimmerman, *Incomes and Expenditures of Minnesota Farm and City Families, 1927-1928*, University of Minnesota, Agricultural Experiment Station, Bulletin 255, June 1929; Jessica B. Peixotto, *Getting and Spending at the Professional Standard of Living* (New York: Macmillan, 1927); Chase Going Woodhouse, "The Standard of Living at the Professional Level, 1816-1817 and 1926-1927," *Journal of Political Economy* 37 (October 1929): 552-572.

10. Hazel Kyrk, *Economic Problems of the Family* (New York: Harper & Brothers, c1929), p. 205; Douglas, *Real Wages in the United States*, p. 391.

11. Kyrk, *Economic Problems of the Family*, p. 193.

12. Helen Humes Lamale, "Changes in Concepts of Income Adequacy over the Last Century," *American Economic Review* (Supplement) 48 (May 1958): 295-296.

13. Florence Nesbitt, *The Chicago Standard Budget for Dependent Families*, Chicago Council of Social Agencies, January 1925, adapted in Thomas D. Eliot, ed., *American Standards and Planes of Living* (New York: Ginn, 1931), pp. 523-539.

14. Lelia Houghteling, *The Income and Standard of Living of Unskilled Laborers in Chicago* (Chicago: University of Chicago Press, 1927), pp. 4-6.

15. Ibid., pp. 129-130.

16. John Modell and Tamara K. Hareven, "Urbanization and the Malleable Household: An Examination of Boarding and Lodging in American Families," *Journal of Marriage and the Family* 35 (August 1973): 467-479.

17. Houghteling, *Income and Standard of Living*, p. 86.

18. Katharine Anthony, "The Family," in H. E. Stearns, ed., *Civilization in the United States* (New York: Harcourt, Brace, 1922), p. 325.

19. Henry L. Lurie, "Economic Stabilization of the Family: The Standard of Living," *National Conference of Social Work*, 1928, p. 291.

20. Karl de Schweinitz, "Are the Poor Really Poor?" *Survey* 59 (Jan. 15, 1928): 517. See also Abraham Epstein, "Have American Wages Permitted an American Standard of Living?" *Annals of the American Academy of Political and Social Science* 97 (September 1921): 169-190.

21. "How the American Middle Class Lives (By One of Them)," *Scribner's Magazine* 86 (December 1929): 694-699; Emily Newall Blair, "Why We Live Beyond Our Means," *Forum* 77 (June 1927): 892-899; Chase Going Woodhouse, "How the Jones Do It," *Survey* 61 (Nov. 1, 1928): 146-150.

22. Anthony, "The Family," p. 325.

23. See Carl O. Taylor, "Changing Rural Standards" and "Where Does the Farmer Get the Standard by Which He Measures His Life and Living?" and Hazel Kyrk, "Cost of Living on Iowa Farms: Household Expenditures," in Eliot, *American Standards*, pp. 705-706, 887-881, 88-102; Carle C. Zimmerman, "The Family Budget as a Tool for Sociological Analysis," *American Journal of Sociology* 33 (1928): 901-911.

24. William E. Leuchtenberg, *The Perils of Prosperity, 1914-1932* (Chicago: University of Chicago Press, 1958), p. 11.

25. David Riesman, *The Lonely Crowd* (New Haven: Yale University Press, 1950).

26. Robert S. Lynd, "The People as Consumers," in President's Research Committee on Social Trends, *Recent Social Trends* (New York: McGraw-Hill, 1933), II, 867.

27. Robert S. Lynd, "Family Members as Consumers," *Annals of the American Academy of Political and Social Science* 160 (1932): 86-93.

28. U.S. Bureau of the Census, Department of Commerce, *Historical Statistics of the United States: Colonial Times to 1957* (Washington, D.C.: Government Printing Office, 1960), p. 526.

29. Charles H. Hession and Hyman Sardy, *Ascent to Affluence: A History of American Economic Development* (Boston: Allyn and Bacon, 1969), p. 670.

30. Ibid., pp. 670-671. See also N. H. Borden, *The Economic Effects of Advertising* (Chicago: Irwin, 1944); W. H. Lough, *High-Level Consumption* (New York: McGraw-Hill, 1935).

31. Stuart Chase, *Prosperity: Fact or Myth?* (New York: C. Doni, 1929), p. 62. See also Chase, "New Standards of Living," *Nation* 129 (Oct. 30, 1929): 488-490.

32. Amy Hewes, "Electrical Appliances in the Home," *Social Forces* 9 (December 1930): 235-242.

33. U.S. Bureau of Labor Statistics, *How American Buying Habits Change* (Washington, D.C.: Government Printing Office, 1959), p. 179.

34. See Lynd, "The People as Consumers," in *Recent Social Trends*, II, 862; John B. Rae, *The American Automobile: A Brief History* (Chicago: University of Chicago Press, 1965), p. 88; Evans Clark, *Financing the Consumer* (New York: Harper & Brothers, 1931).

35. Bureau of Labor Statistics, *How American Buying Habits Change*, p. 183.

36. Ibid., pp. 183-184; Howard F. Bigelow, *Family Finance: A Study in the Economics of Consumption* (Chicago: J. B. Lippincott, 1936), p. 297.

37. "Can Every Family Own a Car?" *Literary Digest* 76 (Feb. 3, 1923): 60-64; "The Little Income and the Big Car," *Literary Digest* 101 (Apr. 27, 1929): 61-63.

38. Earl Chapin May, "My Town and the Motor Car," *Collier's* 75 (Jan. 3, 1925): 17-18; Marsh K. Powers, "The Forgotten Fireside," *Outlook* 130 (Apr. 12, 1922): 608-611.

39. Mildred Maddocks Bentley, "The Housekeeper and Her Car," *Ladies Home Journal* 43 (June 1926): 140-143; Phoebe Cole, "The Auto Solves Some Household Problems," *American Home* 2 (June 1929): 345-; "Friend of the Chil-

dren: The Family Car," *Literary Digest* 92 (Jan. 8, 1927): 65-66.

40. Robert S. Lynd and Helen Merrell Lynd, *Middletown: A Study in American Culture* (New York: Harcourt, Brace & World, 1929), p. 253.

41. Ibid., pp. 254-255. See also "Who Owns a Car," *Literary Digest* 75 (Nov. 11, 1922): 78; Bigelow, *Family Finance*, pp. 298-299.

42. See Kyrk, *Economic Problems of the Family*, p. 367; Elizabeth E. Hoyt, *The Consumption of Wealth* (New York: Macmillan, 1928), pp. 275, 284; Bigelow, *Family Finance*, pp. 299-300.

43. Bigelow, *Family Finance*, p. 301. See also H. I. Phillips, "Newcaritis," *American Magazine* 107 (May 1929): 40-41.

44. E. T. Devine, *The Normal Life* (New York: Survey Associates, 1924), p. 1, quoted in Kyrk, *Economic Problems of the Family*, p. 373.

45. Hazel Kyrk, *A Theory of Consumption* (Boston: 1923). p. 175.

46. Bigelow, *Family Finance*, p. 39.

47. Yandell Henderson and Maurice R. Davie, eds., *Incomes and Living Costs of a University Faculty* (New Haven: Yale University Press, 1928), pp. 7-11.

48. Jessica B. Peixotto, *Getting and Spending at the Professional Standard of Living* (New York: Macmillan, 1927), p. 1.

49. Ibid., p. 40.

50. Quoted in Kyrk, *Economic Problems of the Family*, p. 332.

51. Peixotto, *Getting and Spending*, p. 151.

52. Ibid., pp. 133, and 138.

53. See Kyrk, *Economic Problems of the Family*, p. 367.

54. Peixotto, *Getting and Spending*, p. 133.

55. Ibid., pp. 35-36.

56. Ibid., p. 13.

57. Stuart Chase, "New Standards of Living," *Nation* 129 (Oct. 30, 1929): 488. See also Christine Frederick, "New Wealth, New Standards of Living, and Changed Family Budgets," *Annals of the American Academy of Political and Social Science* 115 (September 1924): 76.

58. Vance Packard, *The Waste Makers* (New York: David McKay, 1960), p. 233.

59. Harold L. Sheppard *et al.*, *Too Old to Work—Too Young to Retire: A Case Study of a Permanent Plant Shutdown*, for the Special Committee on Unemployment Problems, 86th Cong., 1st Sess. (Dec. 21, 1959).

60. Lynd and Lynd, *Middletown*, pp. 80-81.

2. Deficit Living

1. See Frederic S. Mishkin, "The Household Balance Sheet and the Great Depression," *Journal of Economic History* 38 (December 1978): 918-936.

2. Grace Abbott, *From Relief to Social Security: The Development of the New Public Welfare Services and Their Administration* (Chicago: University of Chicago Press, 1941), pp. 4, 72-74. See also Irving Bernstein, *The Lean Years: A History of the American Worker, 1920-1933* (Boston: Houghton Mifflin, 1966), esp. Ch. 1.

3. Robert S. Lynd and Helen M. Lynd, *Middletown in Transition: A Study in Cultural Conflict* (New York: Harcourt, Brace & World, 1937), pp. 14-17.

4. See Glen H. Elder, Jr., *Children of the Great Depression: Social Change in Life Experience* (Chicago: University of Chicago Press, 1974), pp. 3-4; Bernard Sternsher, ed., *Hitting Home: The Great Depression in Town and Country* (Chicago: Quadrangle Books, 1970), pp. 20-21; Eugene Smolensky, *Adjustments to Depression and War, 1930-1945* (Atlanta: Scott, Foresman, 1964), p. 7.

5. National Industrial Conference Board, *The Cost of Living in the United States in 1931* (New York, National Industrial Conference Board, 1932).

6. "Part-Time Work, 13% Wage Cut Shrink Pay Envelopes by 32%," *Business Week*, May 4, 1932, pp. 20-21.

7. See Ewan Clague and Webster Powell, *Ten Thousand Out of Work* (Philadelphia: University of Pennsylvania Press, 1933); Marion Elderton, ed., *Case Studies of Unemployment* (Philadelphia: University of Pennsylvania Press, 1931); Lilian Brandt, *An Impressionistic View of the Winter of 1930-31 in New York City* (New York: Welfare Council of New York City, 1932); J. M. Williams, *Human Aspects of Unemployment and Relief* (Chapel Hill: University of North Carolina Press, 1933); Gladys L. Palmer, *Thirty Thousand Out of Work* (Harrisburg, Pennsylvania, 1933).

8. Ellen S. Woodward, "The Works Progress Administration School Lunch Project," *Journal of Home Economics* 37 (November 1936): 593.

9. Brandt, *An Impressionistic View*, p. 22.

10. Meredith B. Givens, "Statistical Measures of Social Aspects of Unemployment," *Journal of American Statistical Association* 26 (September 1931): 309-310.

11. Ibid., p. 311.

12. "Success Story: The Life and Circumstances of Mr. Gerald Corkum—Paint Sprayman in the Plymouth Motor Plant," *Fortune* 12 (December 1935): 115-120.

13. Clague and Powell, *Ten Thousand Out of Work*, p. 121.

14. Samuel A. Stouffer and Paul E. Lazarsfeld, *Research Memorandum on the Family in the Depression*, Social Science Research Council, Bulletin no. 29 (New York, Social Science Research Council, 1937), pp. 99-100. See also Paul H. Douglas, "The New Deal and the Family: The Administration Moves to Protect the Family Home," *Journal of the American Association of University Women* 28 (October 1934): 9-14.

15. William A. Berridge, "Employment, Unemployment and Related Conditions of Labor," *American Journal of Sociology* 37 (May 1932): 903-904.

16. "Costs More to Live," *Business Week*, Aug. 1, 1936, pp. 28-29; John Janney, "Our Shrinking Dollars," *American Magazine* 124 (July 1937): 24-25. See also *Monthly Labor Review*, which during the 1930s ran a monthly account of the rise or decline in the cost of living with respect to particular commodities.

17. Frank K. Shuttleworth, "The Dollars and Real Income of Teachers, 1889-90 to 1933-34," *School and Society* 39 (May 26, 1934): 683.

18. Elizabeth Ellis Hoyt, *Consumption in Our Society* (New York: McGraw-Hill, 1938), pp. 175-176.

19. National Resources Committee, *Consumer Incomes in the United States: Their Distribution in 1935-36* (Washington, D.C.: Government Printing Office, 1938), p. 2.

20. "Incomes of Families and Single Persons, 1935-1936," *Monthly Labor Review* 47 (October 1938): 728-729.

21. Selma F. Goldsmith, "The Relation of Census Income Distribution Statistics to Other Income Data," in G. Garvy, ed., *An Appraisal of the 1950 Census Data* (Princeton: Princeton University Press, 1958), p. 94.

22. National Resources Committee, *Consumer Incomes in the United States*, p. 41.

23. Ibid., p. 23.

24. Ibid., p. 26.

25. Ibid., p. 26; see also pp. 20-23, 28-29.

26. Hoyt, *Consumption in Our Society*, pp. 177-181.

27. Ibid., pp. 179-181. See also "Effect of the Depression upon the Consumption of Commodities," *Monthly Labor Review* 37 (November 1933): 1090-1092.

28. Faith M. Williams, "Changes in Family Expenditures in the Post-War Period," *Monthly Labor Review* 47 (November 1938): 979.

29. "Where the Consumer Dollar Goes," *Business Week*, July 9, 1938, p. 38.

30. Ibid., p. 977.

31. Faith Williams, "Food Consumption at Different Economic Levels," *Monthly Labor Review* 42 (April 1936): 889-894. See also U.S. Department of Labor, Bureau of Labor Statistics, *Family Expenditures in Selected Cities, 1935-1936*, vol. II, *Food*, Bulletin No. 648 (Washington, D.C.: Government Printing Office, 1940).

32. *Family Expenditures*, vol. I, *Housing*, p. vii.

33. Williams, "Changes in Family Expenditures," p. 977. See also Hoyt, *Consumption in Our Society*, pp. 369-370.

34. Lynd and Lynd, *Middletown*, pp. 266, 26.

35. *Family Expenditures*, vol. VI, *Travel and Transportation*, pp. 3-4; Lynd and Lynd, *Middletown*, p. 573.

36. Lynd and Lynd, *Middletown*, p. 267.

37. *Family Expenditures*, vol. VI, *Travel and Transportation*, pp. 4, 14.

38. Ibid., pp. 11-15.

39. *Family Expenditures*, vol. VII, *Recreation, Reading, Formal Education, Tobacco, Contributions, and Personal Taxes*, p. 80; Williams, "Changes in Family Expenditures," p. 977.

40. *Family Expenditures*, vol. VII, *Recreation*, p. 8.

41. *Family Expenditures*, vol. V, *Medical Care*, p. vii. See also Lynd and Lynd, *Middletown*, pp. 388-401.

42. This idea was suggested by Clarke A. Chambers, who recalls that his father, a small-town doctor during the Depression years, once delivered a baby and was repaid with a puppy. The family also received a steady supply of produce—eggs, butter, cottage cheese, and vegetables—from their neighbor patients during these years. This kind of "barter system," which may have been wide-

spread, suggests that many families were able to survive the Depression simply by relying upon the good will of their neighbors who performed services rather than repaying in cash.

43. *Family Expenditures*, vol. V, *Medical Care*, pp. 6-7; and Day Monroe, "Levels of Living of the Nation's Families," *Journal of Home Economics* 29 (December 1937): 670.

44. Alice O'Reardon Overbeck, "Back to Plain Living," *Forum* 88 (November 1932): 302.

45. Ibid., p. 306.

46. "How We Live on $2,500 a Year," *Ladies' Home Journal* 47 (October 1930): 104. See also H. Thompson Rich, "How to Live Beyond Your Means," *Reader's Digest* 34 (May 1939): 1-4.

47. Helen Peavy Washburn, "We Got Our Money's Worth," *Forum* 96 (November 1936): 200. The argument that Americans had gotten soft was common during the Depression, but it was directed more often at the relief recipient than at the middle-class family. S. Miles Bouton, "The Lion's Mouth: Spoiled by Prosperity," *Harper's Magazine* 171 (November 1935): 761-764, claimed that Americans were spoiled. He felt that people should walk rather than drive cars and that relief in particular should impose a Spartan existence upon its recipients —which indeed it did.

48. "Meeting the Salary Cut," *Commonweal* 15 (Feb. 10, 1932): 407-408.

49. Marion Dunckel Cota, "We Were Only Broke for a Time," *Survey Graphic* 25 (December 1939): 672-673. See also Robert C. Angell, *The Family Encounters the Depression* (New York: Charles Scribner's Sons, 1936).

50. A family budget contest conducted by *Forum* in 1931 illustrates the extent to which the popular journals were out of touch with reality. The contest required a model budget for incomes of $10,000, $7,500, $4,000, and a retirement income of $2,400.

51. "Personal Glimpses: Champion Nickel Stretchers," *Literary Digest* 107 (Jan. 10, 1931): 32-34.

52. *Family Expenditures*, vol. I, *Housing*, pp. 4-5.

53. "Personal Glimpses," pp. 33-34.

54. Josephine Lawrence, *If I Had Four Apples* (New York: Frederick A. Stokes, 1935), p. 13.

55. Ibid., p. 292.

56. Ibid., p. 11-12.

57. Will Cuppy, "I'm Not the Budget Type," *Scribner's Magazine* 102 (December 1937): 19-21.

58. Henry F. Pringle, "What Do the Women of America Think about Money?" *Ladies' Home Journal* 55 (April 1938): 100.

59. Duncan McC. Holthausen *et al.*, *The Volume of Consumer Installment Credit, 1929-1938* (New York: National Bureau of Economic Research, 1940), p. 11.

60. Pringle, "What Do the Women of America Think about Money?" p. 100.

61. Blanche Bernstein, *The Pattern of Consumer Debt, 1935-36* (New York: National Bureau of Economic Research, 1940), pp. 10, 113-116.

62. Ibid., p. 10; Lynd and Lynd, *Middletown*, p. 203. See also Gottfried Haberler, *Consumer Installment Credit and Economic Fluctuations* (New York: National Bureau of Economic Research, 1942).

63. Earle Edward Eubank, "A Case Study of the Effects of Consumer Credit upon the Family," *Annals of the American Academy of Political and Social Science* 196 (March 1936): 220.

64. See Ruth Milkman, "Women's Work and Economic Crisis: Some Lessons of the Great Depression," *Review of Radical Political Economics* 8 (Spring 1976): 73-97.

65. Chase Going Woodhouse, "Managing the Money in Successful Families," *Journal of Home Economics* 23 (January 1931): 1-8.

66. "That Family Budget," *The Survey* 69 (April 1933): 161. See also Burr Blackburn, "Should the Wife Control the Family Purse?" *American Magazine* 116 (September 1933): 106-107.

67. Betty Thornley Stuart, "The Woman Spends," *Collier's* 86 (Oct. 4, 1930): 30.

68. Lawrence, *If I Had Four Apples*, pp. 96-102.

69. Mrs. Ralph Borsodi, "What Should the Home Contribute?" *Journal of Home Economics* 28 (June 1936): 365-367. See also Ralph Borsodi, *This Ugly Civilization* (New York: Simon and Schuster, 1929); Borsodi, *Education and Living* (New York, Devin-Adair, 1948); Borsodi, *The Distribution Age* (New York: D. Appleton, 1927); Borsodi, *Flight from the City* (New York: Harper & Row, 1933).

70. See *Family Expenditures*, vol. II, *Food*, p. 76.

71. Mrs. Borsodi, "What Should the Home Contribute?" p. 367.

3. Mothers and Children

1. See John Modell, Frank F. Furstenburg, Jr., and Theodore Hershberg, "Social Change and Transitions to Adulthood in Historical Perspective," *Journal of Family History*, Autumn 1976, pp. 7-32; Joseph F. Kett, *Rites of Passage: Adolescence in America, 1790 to the Present* (New York: Basic Books, Publishers, 1977).

2. See Wilson H. Grabill, Clyde V. Kiser, and Pascal K. Welpton, "A Long View," in Michael Gordon, ed., *The American Family in Social-Historical Perspective* (New York: St. Martin's Press, 1973), p. 384; U.S. Department of Commerce, Bureau of the Census, *Statistical Abstract of the United States: 1968* (Washington, D.C.: Government Printing Office, 1968), p. 47; Warren S. Thompson and P. K. Whelpton, *Population Trends in the United States* (New York: McGraw-Hill, 1933), p. 263.

3. See Nancy Pottisham Weiss, "Mother, the Invention of Necessity: Dr. Benjamin Spock's *Baby and Child Care*," *American Quarterly* 29 (Winter 1977): 519-546.

4. Samuel A. Stouffer and Paul F. Lazarsfeld, *Research Memorandum on the Family in the Depression* (New York: Social Science Research Council, 1937), pp. 137-138. See also Linda Gordon, *Woman's Body, Woman's Right: Birth Control in America* (New York: Penguin Books, 1977); David M. Kennedy, *Birth*

Control in America: The Career of Margaret Sanger (New Haven: Yale University Press, 1970), ch. 6.

5. Norman E. Himes, *Medical History of Contraception* (Baltimore: Williams and Wilkins, 1936), pp. 340-345; see also pp. 357-367.

6. Lawrence K. Frank, "Childhood and Youth," in President's Research Committee in Social Trends, ed., *Recent Social Trends* (New York: McGraw-Hill, 1933), pp. 11, 751-752.

7. John B. Watson, *Psychological Care of Infant and Child* (New York: W. W. Norton, 1928). See also Gilman M. Ostrander, *American Civilization in the First Machine Age, 1890-1940* (New York: Harper & Row, 1970), pp. 133-134.

8. Ralph P. Bridgman, "Ten Years' Progress in Parent Education," *Annals of the American Academy of Political and Social Science* 151 (1930): 32-45. See also Frank, "Childhood and Youth"; Helen Merrell Lynd, "Parent Education and the College," and Ernest R. Groves, "Parent Education," *Annals* 160 (March 1932): 197-204, 216-222; Phyllis Blanchard, "Status of the Child," *American Journal of Sociology* 35 (1930): 1089.

9. Kett, *Rites of Passage*, chs. 7-8; Roberts S. Lynd and Helen M. Lynd, *Middletown: A Study in Modern American Culture* (New York: Harcourt, Brace & World, 1929), p. 151.

10. Hildegarde Kneeland, "Women's Economic Contribution in the Home," *Annals* 143 (1929): 33-40. See also Kneeland, "Is the Modern Housewife a Lady of Leisure?" *Survey* 62 (1929): 301-302; Chase Going Woodhouse, "The New Profession of Homemaking," *Survey* 57 (December 1926): 316-317; Ruth Schwartz Cowan, "A Case Study of Technological and Social Change: The Washing Machine and the Working Wife," in Mary Hartman and Lois W. Banner, eds., *Clio's Consciousness Raised: New Perspectives on the History of Women* (New York: Harper & Row, 1974), pp. 245-253.

11. William F. Ogburn, "The Family and Its Functions," in *Recent Social Trends*, pp. 1, 669-670.

12. See *Fifteenth Census of the United States: 1930. Population*, vol. VI, *Families* (Washington, D.C.: Government Printing Office, 1933), p. 22; *Sixteenth Census of the United States: 1940. Population and Housing, Families: General Characteristics* (Washington, D.C.: Government Printing Office, 1943), p. 38.

13. See *Fourteenth Census of the United States: 1920. Population*, vol. IV, *Occupations* (Washington, D.C.: Government Printing Office), pp. 20, 22, 23, 475.

14. Katharine DuPre Lumpkin and Dorothy Wolff Douglas, *Child Workers in America* (New York: International Publishers, 1937), pp. 54, 86-87. See also Walter I. Trattner, *Crusade for the Children; A History of the National Child Labor Committee and Child Labor Reform in America* (Chicago: Quadrangle Books, 1970).

15. Unfortunately there is no parallel data for earlier census years, but the 1930 census gives 13.8 percent of families as having a gainfully employed homemaker. Apparently homemakers in 1930 were slightly more apt to be gainfully employed than in 1940, a tendency that contradicts the increase in the proportion

of married working women during the decade. But the two figures are not really comparable, since the 1940 figure is for women with husbands present, and the 1930 figure does not specify the presence of husbands. See *Census of 1930, Population*, vol. VI, *Families*, p. 38.

16. *Sixteenth Census of the United States: 1940. Population. The Labor Force (Sample Statistics), Employment and Personal Characteristics* (Washington, D.C.: Government Printing Office, 1943), p. 137; see also pp. 55, 133.

17. See U.S. Department of Labor, Women's Bureau, *The Share of Wage-Earning Women in Family Support*, Bulletin no. 30 (Washington, D.C.: Government Printing Office, 1923), pp. 77-78, which shows the total contributions to 56 families. In every case, the mother and father contributed all of their earnings to the family. This was true for sons and daughters in only 23 cases. Daughters were much more likely to make a total contribution than were sons.

18. Virginia Yans-McLaughlin, "A Flexible Tradition: South Italian Immigrants Confront a New Work Experience," in Richard L. Ehrlich, ed., *Immigrants in Industrial America, 1850-1920* (Charlottesville: University of Virginia Press, 1977), pp. 74-77; Tamara K. Hareven, "Family and Work Patterns of Immigrant Laborers in a Planned Industrial Town, 1900-1930," in Ehrlich, ed., *Immigrants*, pp. 62-63. See also Claudia Goldin, "Household and Market Production of Families in a Late Nineteenth Century American City," *Explorations in Economic History* 16 (April 1979): 115-116.

19. Helen Sumner Woodbury, *The Working Children of Boston: A Study of Child Labor under a Modern System of Legal Regulation*, U.S. Department of Labor, Children's Bureau, Publication no. 89 (Washington, D.C.: Government Printing Office, 1922); *Child Labor and the Welfare of Children in an Anthracite Coal-Mining District*, U.S. Department of Labor, Children's Bureau, Bulletin no. 106 (Washington, D.C.: Government Printing Office, 1922), pp. 13-14. See also *Minors in Automobile and Metal Manufacturing Industries in Michigan*, Publication no. 126 (1923); *Work of Children on Truck and Small-Farms in Southern New Jersey*, Publication no. 132 (1924); *Child Labor in North Dakota*, Publication no. 129 (1923); *Child Labor and the Work of Mothers in the Beet Fields of Colorado and Michigan*, Publication no. 115 (1923).

20. *Fifteenth Census of the United States: 1930. Population*. vol. V. *General Report on Occupations* (Washington, D.C.: Government Printing Office, 1933), p. 347.

21. See Joseph A. Hill, *Women in Gainful Occupations, 1870-1920*, Census Monographs, IX (Washington, D.C.: Government Printing Office, 1929), p. 78. See also Yans-McLaughlin, "A Flexible Tradition"; Caroline Golab, "The Impact of the Industrial Experience on the Immigrant Family: The Huddled Masses Reconsidered," in Ehrlich, ed., *Immigrants*, pp. 1-32; Barbara Klaczynska, "Why Women Work: A Comparison of Various Groups— Philadelphia, 1910-1930," *Labor History* 17 (Winter 1976): 73-87; Leslie Woodcock Tentler, *Wage-Earning Women: Industrial Work and Family Life in the United States, 1900-1930* (New York: Oxford University Press, 1979).

22. See Kett, *Rites of Passage*, pp. 144-172. A study of working mothers in 1925 indicated that 38 percent worked to allow their families a standard of living beyond subsistence, and 37 percent had children attending parochial schools.

Gwendolyn Salisbury Hughes, *Mothers in Industry: Wage Earning Mothers in Philadelphia* (New York, 1925), pp. 36-42, 52-60, 140. See also Barbara Klaczynska, "Why Women Work: A Comparison of Various Groups—Philadelphia, 1910-1930," *Labor History* 17 (Winter 1976): 77.

4. The Married Woman Worker

1. Mary Anderson, *Woman at Work* (Minneapolis: University of Minnesota Press, 1949), p. 139.

2. See e.g. *The Share of Wage-Earning Women in Family Support*, Women's Bureau, Bulletin no. 41, 1925; *What the Wage-Earning Woman Contributes to Family Support*, Women's Bureau, Bulletin no. 75, 1929. See also Gwendolyn Salisbury Hughes, *Mothers in Industry: Wage-earning by Mothers in Philadelphia* (New York: New Republic, 1925); Helen Glenn Tyson, "Mothers Who Earn," *Survey* 57 (Dec. 1, 1926): 275-279; Eleanor G. Coit and Elsie D. Harper, "Why Do Married Women Work?" *Survey* 64 (April 1930): 79-80.

3. "From Our Readers to Our Readers," *Literary Digest* 116 (Nov. 4, 1933): 2.

4. Ibid., 116 (Dec. 23, 1933): 30.

5. See e.g. Ruth Shallcross, "Portrait of a Working Wife," *Independent Woman* 19 (August 1940): 234-235; Helen Buckler, "Shall Married Women Be Fired?" *Scribner Magazine* 91 (March 1932): 166-168; Edna C. Knight, "Jobs—For Men Only? Shall We Send the Women Workers Home?" *Outlook* 159 (Sept. 2, 1931): 12.

6. See e.g. Howard Dozier, "Women and Unemployment," *Review of Reviews* 85 (March 1932): 55-56; Rita Halle, "Do You Need Your Job?" *Good Housekeeping* 95 (September 1932): 24-25; Frank L. Hopkins, "Should Wives Work?" *American Mercury* 39 (December 1936): 409-416.

7. Weir Jepson, "Save the Home," *American Federationist* 40 (December 1933): 1369-1371.

8. Katharine Anthony, *Mothers Who Must Earn* (New York: Russell Sage Foundation, 1914).

9. See e.g. U.S. Department of Labor, Women's Bureau, *The Family Status of Breadwinning Women*, Bulletin no. 23 (Washington, D.C.: Government Printing Office, 1922); Agnes L. Peterson, "What the Wage-Earning Woman Contributes to Family Support," *Annals of the American Academy of Political and Social Science* 160 (March 1932), pp. 79-80.

10. Eleanor G. Coit and Elsie D. Harper, "Why Do Married Women Work?" *Survey* 64 (Apr. 15, 1930): 79-80.

11. See Alice Kesseler-Harris, "Women's Wage Work as Myth and History," *Labor History* 19 (Spring 1978): 287-307.

12. Frances R. Donovan, *The Saleslady* (Chicago: University of Chicago Press, 1929), pp. 138, 216-217, p. 177.

13. Lorine Pruette, "The Married Woman and the Part-time Job," *Annals of the American Academy of Political and Social Science* 143 (1929): 301-306; Lois Scharf, "Marriage and Careers: Feminism in the 1920s," paper presented to Conference on the History of Women, sponsored by Women Historians of the Mid-

west, at the College of St. Catherine, St. Paul, Minn., Oct. 24-25, 1975.

14. Virginia MacMakin Collier, *Marriage and Careers: A Study of One Hundred Women Who Are Wives, Mothers, Homemakers, and Professional Workers*, Bureau of Vocational Information (New York: Channel Bookstore, 1926), pp. 13, 49-51.

15. Cecile Tipton LaFollette, *A Study of the Problems of 652 Gainfully Employed Married Women Homemakers*, Contributions to Education, no. 619 (New York: Bureau of Publications, Teachers College, Columbia University, 1934), p. 29.

16. Ibid., p. 31.

17. U.S. Department of Labor, Women's Bureau, *The Employed Woman Homemaker in the United States: Her Responsibility for Family Support*, Bulletin no. 148 (Washington, D.C.: Government Printing Office, 1936).

18. U.S. Department of Labor, Bureau of Labor Statistics, *Family Income in Chicago, 1935-36*, Bulletin no. 642, vol. I (Washington, D.C.: Government Printing Office, 1939).

19. "Many Women Support Chicago Families," *The Woman Worker* 19 (July 1939): 5-6.

20. Bureau of Labor Statistics, *Family Income in Chicago*, p. 112.

21. National Federation of Business and Professional Women's Clubs, *Why Women Work*, Public Affairs Pamphlet no. 17 (New York, 1938). See also *The Woman Worker* 18 (May 1938): 14.

22. Ruth Shallcross, "Portrait of the Working Wife," *Independent Woman* 19 (August 1940): 234-235.

23. William F. Ogburn, "The Outlook for the Trained Woman: A Survey of Trends and Prospects," *Journal of the American Association of University Women* 27 (April 1934): 146-152.

24. Helen E. Davis, *Women's Professional Problems in the Field of Education: A Map of Needed Research*, Pi Lambda Theta Studies, no. 1 (New York: Pi Lambda Theta, 1936), p. 13.

25. Sixteenth Census of the United States: 1940. *Family Wage or Salary Income in 1939* (Washington, D.C.: Government Printing Office, 1943), p. 7.

26. Sixteenth Census of the United States: 1940. *The Labor Force*, pt. 1, *U.S. Summary* (Washington, D.C.: Government Printing Office, 1943), p. 116.

27. Sixteenth Census of the United States: 1940. *Population: The Labor Force (Sample Statistics), Employment and Personal Characteristics* (Washington, D.C.: Government Printing Office, 1943), p. 29.

5. Working Women in the Great Depression

1. See W. Elliot Brownlee and Mary M. Brownlee, *Women in the American Economy: A Documentary History, 1675 to 1929* (New Haven: Yale University Press, 1976), pp. 1-39; Alice Kessler-Harris, "Women, Work, and the Social Order" in Berenice A. Carroll, ed., *Liberating Women's History: Theoretical and Critical Essays* (Urbana: University of Illinois Press, 1976), pp. 332-333.

2. National Manpower Council, *Womanpower* (New York: Columbia University Press, 1957), p. 120. See also C. Wright Mills, *White Collar: The*

American Middle Classes (New York: Oxford University Press, 1953), pp. 198-204; Margery Davis, "Woman's Place Is at the Typewriter: The Feminization of the Clerical Labor Force," *Radical America* 8 (July-August 1974): 1-28.

3. Mary V. Dempsey, *The Occupational Progress of Women, 1910 to 1930,* U.S. Department of Labor, Women's Bureau, Bulletin no. 104 (Washington, D.C.: Government Printing Office, 1933), pp. 28-30. Nonetheless, over half of the domestic and personal service workers in 1930 were still in the servant class. The numbers in this group had increased by 62 percent from 1920 to 1930, a development partly related to the migration of Blacks toward the cities of the North and Middle West. The number of black servants increased 81 percent, as compared with a gain of 49 percent among all other service workers. Also, to some extent the overall gain probably reflected a postwar readjustment. Women who had held other jobs during the war returned to domestic service in the subsequent decade, and some who had not worked previously now sought employment in this field.

4. Janet M. Hooks, *Women's Occupations Through Seven Decades,* U.S. Department of Labor, Women's Bureau, Bulletin no. 218 (Washington, D.C.: Government Printing Office, 1947), pp. 78-79.

5. Ibid., p. 89.

6. See Mary Roth Walsh, *"Doctors Wanted: No Women Need Apply": Sexual Barriers in the Medical Profession* (New Haven: Yale University Press, 1977).

7. See e.g. Robert Smuts, *Women and Work in America* (New York: Schocken, 1959), pp. 89-93; Women's Bureau studies of the 1920s and 1930s; Kessler-Harris, "Women, Work, and the Social Order," pp. 334-335.

8. See Valerie Kincade Oppenheimer, *The Female Labor Force in the United States: Demographic and Economic Factors Governing Its Growth and Changing Composition* (Berkeley: Institute of International Studies, University of California, 1969), ch. 3; Ruth Milkman, "Women's Work and Economic Crisis: Some Lessons of the Great Depression," *Review of Radical Political Economics* 8 (Spring 1976): 73-97.

9. Winifred D. Wandersee Bolin, "Past Ideals and Present Pleasures: Women, Work, and Family, 1920-1940," unpub. diss., University of Minnesota, 1976, pp. 102-103.

10. See Lynn Weiner, "A Woman's Place Is in the Home: American Working Women and the Ideology of Domesticity, 1865-1978," diss. in process, Boston University; William L. O'Neill, ed., *Women at Work* (Chicago: Quadrangle Books, 1972); Judith Smith, "The 'New Women' Know How to Type: Some Connections Between Sexual Ideology and Clerical Work, 1900-1930," paper presented at Berkshire Conference on Women's History, Radcliffe, October 1974; Joseph F. Kett, *Rites of Passage: Adolescence in America, 1790 to the Present* (New York: Basic Books, 1977), pp. 150-153; Winifred D. Wandersee Bolin, "The Changing Nature of the Female Labor Force, 1920-1940," paper presented at Conference on the History of Women, sponsored by Women Historians of the Midwest, at College of St. Catherine, St. Paul, Minn., Oct. 24-15, 1975.

11. See Alan L. Sorkin, "On the Occupational Status of Women, 1870-1970," *American Journal of Economics and Sociology* 32 (July 1973): 238-239.

12. See William H. Chafe, *The American Woman: Her Changing Social, Economic, and Political Roles, 1920-1970* (New York: Oxford University Press, 1972), p. 61; Elizabeth Faulkner Baker, *Technology and Woman's Work* (New York: Columbia University Press, 1964), pp. 398-401, 404-411.

13. Margaret H. Hogg, *The Incidence of Work Shortage: Report of a Survey by Sample of Families Made in New Haven, Connecticut, in May-June, 1931* (New York: Russell Sage Foundation, 1932), pp. 24-25.

14. "Findings of the Unemployment Census," *The Woman Worker* 17 (November 1938): 4; Mary E. Pidgeon, *Employment Fluctuations and Unemployment of Women: Certain Indications from Various Sources, 1928-31*, U.S. Department of Labor, Women's Bureau Bulletin no. 113 (Washington, D.C.: Government Printing Office, 1933).

15. Elisabeth D. Benham, *The Woman Wage Earner: Her Situation Today*, U.S. Department of Labor, Women's Bureau Bulletin no. 172 (Washington, D.C.: Government Printing Office, 1939), p. 20. See also U.S. Department of Labor, Women's Bureau, *Office Work and Office Workers in 1940*, Bulletin no. 188 (Washington, D.C.: Government Printing Office, 1942), p. 1; Frances R. Donovan, *The Saleslady* (Chicago: University of Chicago Press, 1929).

16. Benham, *The Woman Wage Earner*, p. 20.

17. Ibid.

18. Ibid., p. 50.

19. Lorine Pruette, *Women Workers Through the Depression* (New York: Macmillan, 1934), pp. 144-145, 21-22.

20. Ibid., pp. 22-23, 126-130.

21. Ibid., pp. 21-22.

22. Mary E. Pidgeon, *Employed Women under N.R.A. Codes*, U.S. Department of Labor, Women's Bureau, Bulletin no. 130 (Washington, D.C.: Government Printing Office, 1935), pp. 7, 31. See also Lois Scharf, " 'The Forgotten Woman': Working Women, The New Deal and Women's Organizations," paper presented at Organization of American Historians, New York, Apr. 17, 1978.

23. William H. Chafe, *The American Woman: Her Changing Social, Economic, and Political Roles, 1920-1970* (New York: Oxford University Press, 1972), pp. 82-83. See also Amy Hewes, "Women Wage-Earners and the N.R.A.," *American Federationist* 41 (February 1935): 164.

24. "Women and the W.P.A.," *The Woman Worker* 18 (September 1938): 8. See also Ellen S. Woodward, "W.P.A.'s Program of Training for Housework," *Journal of Home Economics* 31 (February 1939): 86-88; Florence Kerr, "Training for Household Employment: The W.P.A. Program," *Journal of Home Economics* 32 (September 1940): 437-440.

25. Kerr, "Training for Household Employment," "Women and the W.P.A.," p. 8.

26. "Occupations of W.P.A. Workers," *Monthly Labor Review* 49 (August 1939): 355-356.

27. National Industrial Conference Board, *Women Workers and Labor Supply* (New York, 1936).

28. Mary Anderson, *Woman at Work* (Minneapolis: University of Minnesota Press, 1949), p. 139.

29. Pidgeon, *Employed Women under NRA Codes*, pp. 140-141.

30. Lorine Pruette, *Women Workers Through the Depression* (New York: Macmillan, 1934). See also Ruth Shallcross, *Should Married Women Work?* National Federation of Business and Professional Women's Clubs, Public Affairs Pamphlet no. 49, 1940; Lois Scharf, "Economic Discrimination Against Married Women During the Depression," paper presented at Berkshire Conference on Women's History, Bryn Mawr, Penn., June 10, 1976.

31. Shallcross, *Should Married Women Work?* pp. 5-6; "Work of Married Women Seriously Menaced," *The Woman Worker* 19 (May 1939): 3-4.

32. Anderson, *Woman at Work*, pp. 155-156; Samuel A. Stouffer and Paul E. Lazarsfeld, *Research Memorandum on the Family in the Depression*, Social Science Research Council, Bulletin no. 29 (New York: Social Science Research Council, 1937), p. 56.

33. Shallcross, *Should Married Women Work?* p. 9; "Married Women and Private Industry," *The Woman Worker* 20 (May 1940): 14-15. See also U.S. Department of Labor, Women's Bureau, *Office Work and Office Workers in 1940*, Bulletin no. 188 (Washington, D.C.: Government Printing Office, 1942), pp. 55-57.

34. U.S. Department of Commerce, Bureau of the Census, *Fifteenth Census of the United States, 1930, Population*, vol. V, *General Report on Occupations*, p. 279; *Sixteenth Census of the United States, 1940, The Labor Force*, pt. I, *U.S. Summary*, p. 111.

35. Shallcross, *Should Married Women Work?* pp. 6-7.

36. Pruette, *Women Workers Through the Depression*, pp. 5-6.

37. See Chafe, *The American Woman*, pp. 92-93; Lois Banner, *Women in Modern America: A Brief History* (New York: Harcourt, Brace, Jovanovich, 1974), pp. 191-196; William L. O'Neill, *Everyone Was Brave: A History of Feminism in America* (Chicago: Quadrangle Books, 1969), pp. 264-348.

38. Banner, *Women in Modern America*, p. 196.

6. Women's Place in the Home

1. See Ernest W. Burgess, Harvey J. Locke, and Mary Margaret Thomes, *The Family: From Tradition to Companionship*, 4th ed. (New York: Van Nostrand, 1971); Robert O. Blood and Donald M. Wolfe, *Husbands and Wives: The Dynamics of Married Living* (Glencoe, Ill.: Free Press, 1960); Lois Hoffman, "Effects of the Employment of Mothers on Parental Power Relations and the Division of Household Tasks," *Marriage and Family Living* 22 (February 1960): 27-35; David M. Heer, "Dominance and the Working Wife," *Social Forces* 36 (1958): 341-347; Marvin E. Olsen, "Distribution of Family Responsibility and Social Stratification," *Marriage and Family Living* 22 (February 1960): 60-65; Joseph Veroff and Sheila Feld, *Marriage and Work in America: A Study of Motives and Roles* (New York: Van Nostrand Reinhold, c1970); Ersel E. LeMasters, "The Passing of the Dominant Husband-Father," and Harriet Holter, "Sex Roles and Social Change," in Hans Peter Drietzel, ed., *Recent Sociology No. 4: Family, Marriage, and the Struggle of the Sexes* (New York: MacMillan, 1972).

2. See Margaret M. Poloma and T. Neal Garland, "The Myth of the Egali-

tarian Family: Familial Roles and the Professionally Employed Wife," in Athena
Theodore, ed., *The Professional Woman* (Cambridge, Mass.: Schenkmen, 1971);
Dair L. Gillespie, "Who Has the Power? The Marital Struggle," in Drietzel, ed.,
Recent Sociology, pp. 121-150; William F. Kenkel, "Influence Differentiation in
Family Decision Making," *Sociology and Social Research* 42 (September-October
1957): 18-25; Nicholas Babchuck and Alan P. Bates, "The Primary Relations of
Middle-Class Couples: A Study in Male Dominance," *American Sociological Review* 28 (1963): 377-384.

3. See Lois W. Banner, *Women in Modern America: A Brief History* (New
York: Harcourt Brace Jovanovich, 1974), pp. 151-153; William H. Chafe, *The
American Woman: Her Changing Social, Economic, and Political Roles, 1920-
1970* (New York: Oxford University Press, 1972), pp. 101-103; William L.
O'Neill, *Everyone Was Brave: A History of Feminism in America* (Chicago:
Quadrangle Books, 1969), pp. 302-304; Eleanor Wembridge, "Petting and the
Campus," *Survey* 64 (July 1, 1925): 393.

4. Frances R. Donovan, *The Saleslady* (Chicago: University of Chicago
Press, 1929), pp. 166-167.

5. Phyllis Blanchard and Carolyn Manasses, *New Girls for Old* (New
York: Macaulay, 1937), p. 180, quoted in O'Neill, *Everyone Was Brave*, p. 304.

6. Gillespie, "Who Has the Power?" in Drietzel, ed., *Recent Sociology
No. 4*, pp. 121-150.

7. Poloma and Garland, "The Myth of the Egalitarian Family," in Theodore, ed., *The Professional Woman*, p. 757.

8. Virginia MacMakin Collier, *Marriage and Careers: A Study of One
Hundred Women Who Are Wives, Mothers, Homemakers, and Professional
Workers*, The Bureau of Vocational Information (New York: Channel Bookstore, 1926), pp. 85-87.

9. Cecile Tipton LaFollette, *A Study of the Problems of 652 Gainfully Employed Married Women Homemakers* (New York: Teachers College, Columbia
University 1934), pp. 146-151.

10. See LaFollette, *A Study of the Problems*, p. 146; Collier, *Marriage and
Careers*, pp. 81-85.

11. Hazel Kyrk, *Economic Problems of the Family* (New York: Harper &
Brothers, 1929), pp. 157-158.

12. There are obvious exceptions. In Italian families males were able to
maintain their traditional position of authority despite seasonal unemployment
and economic hardship. Strong cultural traditions sustained male authority,
which was based on more than economic roles. See Virginia McLaughlin, "Patterns of Work and Family Organization: Buffalo's Italians," *Journal of Interdisciplinary History* 2 (Autumn 1971): 299-314.

13. Blood and Wolfe, *Husbands and Wives*, pp. 45-46. See also Mirra Komarovsky, *Blue Collar Marriage* (New York: Vintage Books, c1962), pp. 231-
234. The strong wife-weak husband theme is nevertheless common in American
literature of the twentieth century. See e.g. Betty Smith, *A Tree Grows in Brooklyn* (New York: Harper & Row, 1943).

14. See Ernest Mowrer, *Family Disorganization: An Introduction to a Sociological Analysis* (Chicago: University of Chicago Press, 1929); Mowrer, "Fam-

ily Disorganization and Mobility," *Publications of the American Sociological Society* 23 (1929): 134-145; L. L. Bernard, "The Family in Modern Life," *International Journal of Ethics* 38 (July 1928): 427-442.

15. Samuel A. Stouffer and Paul E. Lazarsfeld, *Research Memorandum on the Family in the Depression,* Social Science Research Council, Bulletin no. 29 (New York: Social Science Research Council, 1937), pp. 28, 36. See also Robert S. Lynd and Helen Merrell Lynd, *Middletown in Transition: A Study in Cultural Conflicts* (New York: Harcourt, Brace & World, 1937), pp. 178-179.

16. Mirra Komarovsky, *The Unemployed Man and His Family: The Effect of Unemployment upon the Status of the Man in Fifty-Nine Families* (New York: Dryden Press, 1940), p. 42.

17. Ibid., pp. 55-58.

18. Ibid., pp. 60-61.

19. Ibid., pp. 38-59.

20. Ibid., pp. 114-115.

21. John French and Berton Raven, "The Bases of Social Power," in Darian Cartwright and Alvin Zander, eds., *Group Dynamics* (New York: Harper & Row, 1968). See also Poloma and Garland, "The Myth of the Equalitarian Family," p. 757.

22. Ruth S. Cavan and Katherine H. Ranck, *The Family and the Depression: A Study of One Hundred Chicago Families* (Chicago: University of Chicago Press, 1938), pp. 1-8, 29-35.

23. Robert C. Angell, *The Family Encounters the Depression* (New York: Charles Scribner's Sons, 1936), pp. 84, 17.

24. Ibid., p. 254; Cavan and Ranck, *The Family and the Depression,* pp. 72-73; Komarovsky, *The Unemployed Man and His Family,* pp. 43-47, 78-82.

25. E. Wight Bakke, *Citizens Without Work: A Study of the Effects of Unemployment upon the Workers' Social Relations and Practices* (New Haven: Yale University Press, 1940), pp. 135-140, 182-184.

26. Ibid., pp. 201-202.

27. E. E. LeMasters, *Blue-Collar Aristocrats: Life-Styles at a Working-Class Tavern* (Madison: University of Wisconsin Press, 1975), pp. 84-85.

28. See Leonard Benson, *Fatherhood: A Sociological Perspective* (New York: Random House, 1968), pp. 148-153.

29. David M. Heer, "The Measurement and Bases of Family Power: An Overview," *Marriage and Family Living* 25 (May 1963): 138.

30. Peter Blau, *Exchange and Power in Social Life* (New York: Wiley, 1964); Benson, *Fatherhood,* pp. 150-151.

31. See Stouffer and Lazarsfeld, *Research Memorandum on the Family,* pp. 149-153.

32. See Komarovsky, *Blue-Collar Marriage;* E. E. LeMaster, *Blue-Collar Aristocrats;* Lee Rainwater, Richard P. Coleman, and Gerald Handel, *Workingman's Wife* (New York: Oceana Publications, 1959); Elizabeth Bott, *Family and Social Network* (New York: Free Press, 1957).

33. Banner, *Women in Modern America,* pp. 191-192.

34. Glenn H. Elder, Jr., *Children of the Great Depression: Social Change in Life Experience* (Chicago: University of Chicago Press, 1974), p. 290.

35. Ibid., pp. 291, 13.
36. Ibid., p. 279.
37. Ibid., p. 282.
38. Ibid., p. 222.

Epilogue

1. See Lois W. Banner, *Women in Modern America: A Brief History* (New York: Harcourt, Brace and Jovanovich, 1974), p. 131; William H. Chafe, *The American Woman: Her Changing Social, Economic, and Political Roles, 1920-1970* (New York: Oxford University Press, 1972), p. 37; William L. O'Neill, *Everyone Was Brave: A History of Feminism in America* (Chicago: Quadrangle Books, 1969), p. 274.

2. Anne Firor Scott, *The Southern Lady: From Pedestal to Politics, 1830-1930* (Chicago: University of Chicago Press, 1970), p. 211.

3. See Banner, *Women in Modern America*, pp. 131-141; Chafe, *The American Woman*, 112-132; O'Neill, *Everyone Was Brave*, pp. 175-286; Clarke A. Chambers, *Seedtime of Reform: American Social Service and Social Action, 1918-1933* (Minneapolis: University of Minnesota Press, 1963), pp. 59-84.

4. J. Stanley Lemons, *The Woman Citizen: Social Feminism in the 1920s* (Chicago: University of Illinois Press, 1973), pp. 234-235.

5. O'Neill, *Everyone Was Brave*, pp. 227-231; Banner, *Women in Modern America*, pp. 146-154; June Sochen, *Movers and Shakers: American Women Thinkers and Activists, 1900-1970* (New York: Quadrangle Books, 1973), pp. 101-103.

6. O'Neill, *Everyone Was Brave*, pp. 273-274, 328, 352-353.

7. Ibid., pp. 325-329, 358.

8. See Lois Scharf, "Marriage and Careers: Feminism in the 1920s," a paper presented at Conference on the History of Women, sponsored by Women Historians of the Midwest, at College of St. Catherine, St. Paul, Minn., Oct. 24-25, 1975; Scharf, "Economic Discrimination Against Married Women During the Depression," paper presented at Berkshire Conference on Women's History, June 10, 1976. Scharf, " 'The Forgotten Woman': Working Women, the New Deal and Women's Organizations," paper presented at Organization of American Historians, Apr. 17, 1979, discusses the position of radical feminists on economic discrimination against the married woman worker and their acceptance of the expediency arguments of the social feminists. Alice Kessler-Harris, "Women's Wage Work as Myth and History," *Labor History* 19 (Spring 1978): 287-307, notes the historical constancy of the expediency argument, and historians' general acceptance of it. Frank Stricker, "Cookbooks and Law Books: The Hidden History of Career Women in Twentieth Century America," *Journal of Social History* 10 (Fall 1976): 1-19, points to women's continued interest in professional and business careers. He feels that the disillusionment of the interwar years has been overstated and misinterpreted. For women's activities in the peace movement, see Joan M. Jensen, "All Pink Sisters: The War Department and the Feminist Movement in the 1920s," paper presented at Fourth Berkshire Conference on the History of Women, Mount Holyoke College, Aug. 23-25, 1978.

9. Charlotte Perkins Gilman, *The Home: Its Work and Influence* (New York: McClure, Phillips, 1903); Gilman, *Women and Economics: A Study of the Economic Relations Between Men and Women as a Factor in Social Evolution* (Boston: Small, Maynard, 1898); Juliet Mitchell, *Women's Estate* (New York: Vintage Books, 1971). See also Ellen Dubois, "The Radicalism of the Woman Suffrage Movement: Notes Toward the Reconstruction of Nineteenth-Century Feminism," *Feminists Studies* 3 (Fall 1975): 63-71.

10. See Patricia Branca, "A New Perspective on Women's Work: A Comparative Typology," *Journal of Social History* 9 (Winter 1975): 129-153; Branca, *Silent Sisterhood: Middle Class Women in the Victorian Home* (London: Croom Helm, 1975); Daniel Scott Smith, "Family Limitation, Sexual Control, and Domestic Feminism in Victorian America," in Mary Hartman and Lois W. Banner, eds., *Clio's Consciousness Raised: New Perspectives on the History of Women* (New York: Harper & Row, 1974), pp. 119-136.

Appendix A

1. Paul A. David and Peter Solar, "A Bicentenary Contribution to the History of the Cost of Living in America," in Paul Uselding, ed., *Research in Economic History: An Annual Compilation of Research*, vol. 2 (Greenwich, Conn.: AiJai Press, 1977), pp. 16-17.

Appendix B

1. Rolf Nugent, *Consumer Credit and Economic Stability* (New York: Russell Sage Foundation, 1939), p. 92.

2. Ibid., pp. 103-105.

3. Ibid., pp. 105-107.

4. Blanche Bernstein, *The Pattern of Consumer Debt, 1935-36: A Statistical Analysis* (New York: National Bureau of Economic Research, 1940), pp. 4-5.

Appendix C

1. Raymond W. Goldsmith, *A Study of Saving in the United States*, II, *Nature and Derivation of Annual Estimates of Saving, 1897-1949* (Princeton: Princeton University Press, 1955), pp. 3-11.

2. Dorothy S. Brady, "Family Saving, 1888 to 1950," in Goldsmith, *A Study of Saving in the United States*, vol. III, *Special Studies*, pp. 140-141.

Appendix D

1. Alba M. Edwards, *Sixteenth Census of the United States: 1940. Population. Comparative Occupation Statistics for the United States, 1870-1940* (Washington, D.C.: Government Printing Office, 1943).

2. Robert W. Smuts, "The Female Labor Force: A Case Study in the Interpretation of Historical Statistics," *Journal of the American Statistical Association* 55 (March 1960): 71-79.

3. A. J. Jaffee, "Trends in the Participation of Women in the Working Force," *Monthly Labor Review* 79 (May 1956): 559-560.

Appendix E

1. *Fifteenth Census of the United States: 1930. Population.* vol. V, *General Report on Occupations* (Washington, D.C.: Government Printing Office, 1933), p. 45.

Index

Abbot, Grace, 27
Advertising, 16, 25
American Federationist, 69
American Woman's Association, 94
Anderson, Mary, 67
Angell, Robert C., 109-110
Agricultural Adjustment Act, 32
Anthony, Katherine, 13, 14, 70
Anthony, Susan B., 120
Automobile, 18-21; attitudes toward, 19-20; and consumer credit, 18; during the Depression, 37, 41-43; and family budget, 20, 23; mass production of, 18; numbers, 19

Bakke, C. Wight, 111-112
Banner, Lois, 119
Birth control, 56
Birth rate, 55-56
Blau, Peter, 114
Blood, Robert, 106
Boarding and lodging, 12-13
Borsodi, Mrs. Ralph, 53-54
Brandt, Lilian, 30
Brookings Institution, 9, 33
Bureau of Labor Statistics: consumer purchases, 36-41; medical care, 44; wage-earners, 75
Bureau of Municipal Research, 13, 14
Blackburn, Burr, 52
Business Week study on national income and expenditures, 23

Cavan, Ruth, 109, 110, 111
Census figures (1910 and 1920), 130-131
Chase, Stuart, 17
Chicago: auto ownership, 42; cost of living, 38; standard budget, 11-12; wage-earners, 75
Child labor: of blacks, 61-62; decline of, 3, 55-56, 61, 102; occupational characteristics of, 62-63; relation to working women, 66, 102. *See also* Ethnicity
Children, 55-58, 114; and the Depression, 29, 111, 113, 115-116
Children's Bureau, 65
Clerical work, 86; during the Depression, 92; and NRA codes, 95-96. *See also* Women workers
Collier, Virginia MacMakin, 72-73, 105
Committee for Industrial Organization (CIO), 96
Committee on Family Social Work, 11-12
Conjugal power, 113-114
Consumer credit, 14, 126-127; and the automobile, 18; during the Depression, 50-51; in lower income families, 50-51
Consumer expenditures, 39-41; on medical care, 44. *See also* Automobile
Consumer prices, 125
Consumer products, 16-18, 126. *See also* Automobile
Consumer Purchases Study, 37-41, 127
Consumerism, 14-18; attitudes toward, 48-49; during the Depression, 36-45; and the family, 24-26; miscellaneous expenditures, 43-44
Corkum, Gerald, 30. *See also* Family: kinship system
Cost of living, 125; during the Depression, 32-33; in New England, 38. *See also* Chicago; New York City

Cuppy, Will, 49

Davis, Helen E., 76
De Schweinitz, Karl, 13-14
Department Store Economist, 100
Devine, E. T., 21
Donovan, Frances, 72, 104
Douglas, Paul H., 9-10

Economic need, 3; definition of, 26;
  during the Depression, 37; and
  women's work, 54, 59, 77, 83, 102
Economy of abundance, 15
Edwards, Alba M., 130
Elder, Glenn, 115-116
Engel's law on consumption and ex-
  penditure, 23
Equal Right's Amendment, 5, 101, 119,
  120
Ethnicity: and child labor, 65; and
  families, 110; and women's work, 66

Fair Labor Standards Act, 95
Family: and the automobile, 19-20;
  budgets, 9-13, 45-49; consumption,
  16, 76; deficit spending, 128-129;
  demographic trends, 114; and the Depression, 26; disorganization, 107,
  110-112; economics, 1, 3, 59-60, 102;
  expenditures and savings, 129; housing, 40-41; and industrialization, 7;
  kinship system, 30-31; matriarchal,
  108, 112; medical care, 44; middle-
  class, 14; middle-income, 59-60;
  patriarchal, 103, 108; and relief policies, 31; roles in, 55, 103-113; rural,
  35; values, 110, 114, 117. *See also*
  Consumption; Great Depression;
  Marriage; Wage-earners
Federal Economy Act, 99
Feminism, 4-5, 101; careerist perspective of, 121; decline of, 118-122; and
  family life, 122; radical, 119-120;
  social, 119, 120; women's attitude
  toward, 104, 116-117, 118, 121
French, John, 109

Garland, T. Neal, 105
Gillespie, Dair L., 104
Gilman, Charlotte Perkins, 121
Goldin, Claudia, 65
Goldsmith, Raymond, 129

Goldsmith, Selma F., 35
Great Depression: children in, 115-116;
  and companionship marriage, 114;
  and families, 26, 27-54, 109-112; and
  family roles, 107-113, 115-116; and
  men, 111; and professional women,
  94-95; psychological impact of, 28;
  and women workers, 4, 84, 89-90,
  102

Hareven, Tamara, 65
Heer, David, 113-114
Hogg, Margaret H., 91
Holyoke Home Information Center, 17.
  See also Mount Holyoke College
Home economics movement, 8
Houghteling, Leila, 12-13
Household Finance Corporation, 52
Household Service Demonstration
  Project, 96

Income, 8-11; distribution, 10, 34-36;
  during the Depression, 28-29, 32-35;
  in 1939, 77; of middle class, 14; of
  unskilled laborers, 12, 14. *See also*
  Wages
International Labor Office, 75

Jaffee, A. J., 131

Kneeland, Hildegarde, 33
Komarovsky, Mirra, 107-108, 110, 111
Kryk, Hazel, 10, 62; on standard of liv-
  ing, 21

Ladies' Home Journal, 46, 50
LaFollette, Cecile, 73-74, 105
LaFollette, Suzanne, 120
Lawrence, Josephine (*If I had Four
  Apples*), 48-49, 53
Lazarsfeld, Paul, 107
LeMaster, E. E., 113, 115
Lemons, J. Stanley, 119
Leuchtenberg, William E., 15
Literary Digest, 47, 69
Lynd, Helen Merrill. *See* Lynd, Robert
  S.
Lynd, Robert S., 15-16; and Helen Mer-
  rill (*Middletown*), 19-20, 25, 28, 41,
  51, 57

Marriage: "companionship," 4, 103-

106, 108, 115, 122; husband's role in,
105-107; and money management,
51-52; women's attitude toward, 104,
119. *See also* Women workers,
married
Men, 113. *See also* Family: roles in;
Great Depression; Marriage: "companionship"; Unemployment
Mitchell, Juliet, 121
Monthly Labor Review, 34, 125
Mount Holyoke College, 16-17

National Bureau of Economic Research,
50
National Conference of Social Work, 13
National Education Association, 99
National Federation of Business and
Professional Women's Club, 75-76,
99, 100
National Industrial Conference Board,
28, 29, 100; *Women Workers and the
Labor Supply*, 97
National Industrial Relations Act
(NIRA), 96
National Recovery Act (NRA): codes,
95; impact on women, 95-96, 98
Nesbitt, Florence, 11
New Bedford, Massachusetts, 92
New Deal, 84; and women workers,
95-97
New England Telephone and Telegraph
Company, 99
New Haven, Connecticut, 91
New York City, 70, 94; auto ownership
in, 42; cost of living, 38
Nineteenth Amendment, 118, 119
Northern Pacific Railroad Company, 99

Occupational classification, 132
Ogburn, William, 9, 58, 76
O'Neill, William, 104, 119-121

Packard, Vance, 25
Parent education, 57
Peixotto, Jessica, 22-24
Philadelphia: Emergency Work Bureau,
31; Family Society of, 13; Society for
Organizing Charity, 13; unemployed
in, 30
"Pin-money" theory, 67, 98
Poloma, Margaret M., 105
Powell, Webster, 31

Progressive Era, 10-11
Prosperity, 7-8
Pruette, Lorine, 72, 94, 101
Public opinion, 2

Ranck, Katherine H., 109
Raven, Bertram, 109
Relief: agencies, 30; families receiving,
35-36
Riesman, David, 15
Russell Sage Foundation, 70

Scott, Anne Firor, 118
Sex roles and labor market segregation,
87-88
Shallcross, Ruth, 76
Sheppard, Harold L., 25
Smuts, Robert, 130-131
Sochen, June, 119
Social power, 109
Social Science Research Council: study
of family relations, 107; study of
gasoline consumption, 41
Social workers, 13
Standards of living: American, 1, 7-8;
and the automobile, 20-21; defini-
tions of, 1, 21, 24; during the Depres-
sion, 38; middle-class, 14; profes-
sional, 22, 24; rural, 14-15; at Univer-
sity of California, Berkeley, 22; of
Yale University faculty, 21-22
Stanton, Elizabeth Cady, 120
Stouffer, Samuel A., 107

Unemployment: coal-miners, 27; during the Depression, 30, 91; impact on
the family, 107-113; impact on men,
107-109, 111-112; middle-class, 47;
professional women, 93-94; saleswomen, 93; women, 91-94
United Charities of Chicago, 11
United States Department of Agriculture, 53
United States Department of Labor, 19,
24
United States Employment Service, 92,
93
United States Rubber Company, 30
University of California, Berkeley, 22

Wage-earners, 26; supplementary, 59-
61, 66, 102

Wages, 13-14; and women's work, 77-81

Watson, John B. (*Psychological Care of Infant and Child*), 57

Williams, Faith, 38-39

Woman Worker, 75

Woman's Party, 119

Women: adaptation to industrialization, 122; attitudes of, 104, 121; authority in the family, 111-115; black, 2, 74; as consumers, 14, 51; as homemakers, 3-4, 53-54, 58-59, 111-112; as money managers, 51-52; as mothers, 3, 55, 56-58; southern, 118. *See also* Women workers

Women workers, 1, 54, 59, 75; agricultural, 86, 95, 130; attitude toward, 67-70, 73, 97-98; black, 1, 74, 83; career women, 69, 72-73, 75; domestic and personal service, 86, 95, 96; in manufacturing, 86; by marital condition, 68; occupational distribution, 84-90; part-time, 72, 92-93; professional work, 87; saleswork, 99, 104; single, 100, 101; supplementary wage-earners, 59-61; values, 83, 101, 102; white collar and clerical, 84, 86-87, 97, 99.

—married, 4, 26, 67, 89; discrimination against, 98-101; husband's income, 73-74, 77-81; husband's occupation, 81-82; reasons for working, 71-74

Women's Bureau, 67, 75, 92; and economic need, 70-71, 74; study of occupational distribution, 86-87

Women's history, 120-121

Women's movement, 5

Women's suffrage, 118-119

Work, nature of, 25

Works Progress Administration (WPA), 99; school lunch projects, 29; and women workers, 92, 96-97

Yale University, 21-22

Yans-McLauglin, Virginia, 65

Youth: education of, 66; employment of, 62-63; family responsibility, 64. *See also* Child labor

YWCA, 71